Praise for *Questioning*

Buy a dozen copies of this book and give them away to all those friends of yours who have ever asked, "Have you got a clear, easy-to-read book that explains the Christian faith in a way that makes sense to someone like me?" because this warm, winsome retelling of the Christian story by two down-to-earth guys fits the bill perfectly.

MICHAEL FROST
Author and speaker, Morling College, Sydney

I'm confident *Questioning Christianity* will stretch and encourage all who read it.

SAM ALLBERRY
Author and speaker; editor for The Gospel Coalition

Dan and Rian have written a thoughtful and helpful book. As apologetic questions continue to shift with emerging generations, they give both fresh and potent answers to the longings of our world today. I am sure this will help many.

JON TYSON
Author of *Beautiful Resistance*; pastor of Church of the City, NYC

Do you have questions about Christianity? You are not alone. And in this wonderful book, Dan and Rian winsomely retell the biblical story with a view from the air and a view from the ground that makes complex truths clear and accessible. Whether you are outright skeptical, or a new Christian seeking to better understand the story that has begun to make sense of why you are on this earth, *Questioning Christianity* is the book that I want to put into your hands.

ADAM RAMSEY
Lead Pastor at Liberti Church, Gold Coast, Australia; Network Director for Acts 29 Australia & New Zealand; author, *Truth on Fire*

With warmth and wit, Dan and Rian have written *Questioning Christianity* to help us navigate life's deepest questions and reflect on the possibility that Jesus offers the world real and tangible hope. Read it and share it with others—I think this book could become a classic of our time.

AMY ORR-EWING
Bestselling author and speaker; President of the OCCA (The Oxford Centre for Christian Apologetics)

What does life mean? Where am I going? *Is there a better story than the one I'm being told?* If these are the questions that you're asking, then please read *Questioning Christianity* by Dan Paterson and Rian Roux. This is a comprehensive, nuanced, and yet easy-to-read overview of the better story that Jesus offers all of us. This story offers us freedom, hope, and forgiveness.

SAM CHAN
Public speaker for City Bible Forum, Australia; author of *Evangelism in a Skeptical World* and *How to Talk About Jesus (Without Being That Guy)*

QUESTIONING CHRISTIANITY

Is there more to the story?

DAN PATERSON
RIAN ROUX

MOODY PUBLISHERS

CHICAGO

Published in association with the literary agency of Wolgemuth and Associates, 7198 S. Little River Court, Aurora, CO 80016.

Interior design: Brandi Davis
Cover design: Charles Brock
Cover illustration of Jesus copyright © 2019 by Iknuitsin Studio / iStock (1133238513). All rights reserved.

All websites and phone numbers listed herein are accurate at the time of publication but may change in the future or cease to exist. The listing of website references and resources does not imply publisher endorsement of the site's entire contents. Groups and organizations are listed for informational purposes, and listing does not imply publisher endorsement of their activities.

Library of Congress Cataloging-in-Publication Data

Names: Paterson, Dan, author. | Roux, Rian, author.
Title: Questioning Christianity : is there more to the story? / Dan
    Paterson and Rian Roux.
Description: Chicago : Moody Publishers, [2021] | Includes bibliographical
    references. | Summary: "Questioning Christianity explores the Christian
    story in an accessible way. No slogans. No politics. No simple solutions
    to complex problems. After years of exploring faith issues with
    skeptics, seekers, and new believers, Dan Paterson and Rian Roux can
    help you navigate what can often be a disorienting journey"-- Provided
    by publisher.
Identifiers: LCCN 2020057838 (print) | LCCN 2020057839 (ebook) | ISBN
    9780802421548 (paperback) | ISBN 9780802499219 (ebook)
Subjects: LCSH: Apologetics.
Classification: LCC BT1103 .P374 2021 (print) | LCC BT1103 (ebook) | DDC
    239--dc23
LC record available at https://lccn.loc.gov/2020057838
LC ebook record available at https://lccn.loc.gov/202005783089

Originally delivered by fleets of horse-drawn wagons, the affordable paperbacks from D. L. Moody's publishing house resourced the church and served everyday people. Now, after more than 125 years of publishing and ministry, Moody Publishers' mission remains the same—even if our delivery systems have changed a bit. For more information on other books (and resources) created from a biblical perspective, go to www.moodypublishers .com or write to:

Moody Publishers
820 N. LaSalle Boulevard
Chicago, IL 60610

1 3 5 7 9 10 8 6 4 2

Printed in the United States of America

To my mentor, Dave, who has gone before me as an endless source
of wisdom, inspiration, and encouragement.
To my father, John, whose shadow looms large over me
as a paragon of sacrifice, devotion, and generosity.
To my wife, Erin, who walks beside me as a beautiful model
of faith, hope, and love.
To my boys who come after me: Josiah, Zachariah, and Seth,
may you leave an indelible footprint on the world
with your sensitivity, courage, and passion.

Dan Paterson

To my family.
To my wife, Sally, your love and partnership
in all things is unwavering.
To our children, Maggie, Theodore, and William,
you fill our lives with joy.
To our parents, your constant love is humbling beyond words.
To our siblings and their partners, you have walked
with us every step of the way.
I am eternally grateful.

Rian Roux

Contents

Why Read This Book?

I can only answer the question "What am I to do?" if I can answer the prior question "Of what story or stories do I find myself a part?"

ALASDAIR MACINTYRE
AFTER VIRTUE

A BETTER STORY

We have this sense—do we not?—call it an inkling, that we are all in the midst of something greater. Humans are inherently story-telling creatures. We try to bring order out of chaos, or make sense of our messy lives, by weaving together the various experiences and ideas we pick up along the way into a bigger story. Whether mythic or scientific, street-level or academic, our world is a swirl of these stories, all competing for our affections and allegiance. Journalists and celebrities, politicians and philosophers, Hollywood and holy people—everyone is spinning a tale of who we are, why we are here, and what we should be chasing to arrive at the elusive *there* of success, fulfilment, enlightenment, or happiness.

Much like a fish is unaware of the water in which it swims, rarely are we even aware of the story we have come to inhabit. Yet the scripts we adopt, consciously or not, act as a lens through which we view the world, shaping every facet of our lives. Embedded into our psyche, these stories inform our choices and govern the kinds of people we become, along with the cultures we go on to create. Given that these stories carry so much power, should we not pause a moment to ponder whether the story we currently inhabit is worth believing?

What if there is a better story—one that when you read its pages, it were as if a new sun dawned, shedding light on the full gamut of our human experience? A story that gave voice to our deepest intuitions, desires, and hopes, with a redemptive power to breathe new life into a weary or wayward soul, even aiding us to stumble toward who we know we are meant to be. A story that helps us reconnect with our life's true purpose, so when we step into its pages, taking on the script for ourselves, all of life is animated with new meaning.

We believe such a story exists. A compelling narrative that emerges across the various scenes of the Bible, which serves as something of a grand archetype to which other good stories are merely echoes. This is God's story, or what we will call the Christian story from now on, with Jesus of Nazareth as the central character. In light of who He is and what He teaches, all of us are invited to rethink the stories we inhabit and to reimagine what life could look like with God as the Author of our script.

QUESTIONING THE STORY

There may be readers who found that last paragraph rather percussive, a terrible anticlimax to what seemed at first an exciting invitation to join the search for meaning. After all, hasn't the Christian story been tried and found wanting, with any beautiful words being hollowed out by the deeply flawed history of the Church? And hasn't the secular world moved beyond ancient fairytales?

Serious challenges assault the credibility of the Christian story, provoking doubts even for lifelong believers. There is no skirting the reality that hard questions need to be asked of Christianity, and later we will give voice to these concerns. At the outset, though, we want to flag the possibility that things may not be quite what they seem. That perhaps the origin of our own doubts could be less of a problem with the relevance or reasonableness of the story itself and more to do with the shortcomings of its broadcasters.

The danger with all stories that journey through the generations is that they tend to accumulate cultural baggage. We hear the message not as it was first given but filtered through the voices of later storytellers who have too often wandered off script or through critics with a penchant for caricature. This can lead us to reject the Christian story not for what it is, but for what we have seen and heard from others.

Consider the tragedy of this modern parable.

There were once two parents who unknowingly gave their toddler a drink made from soured milk. "Here," they said, "have a chocolate milkshake!" The child had never tasted one before, so intrigued, they took a giant gulp from the oversized cup. As the horrendous taste registered on their tongue, the child recoiled in disgust, deciding they would rather poke themselves in the eye than endure a second sip. As the child grew, traumatized by this early culinary memory, they were shocked that stores could successfully market this dreadful torture of the tastebuds. They simply couldn't understand their friends' excitement at the mere suggestion of a milkshake, let alone return to the cup for another taste themselves.

The obvious point of this parable is that the child misses out on ever tasting a delicious milkshake because of an unfortunate history of misrepresentation. And what is true of a misrepresented drink can also be true of a misrepresented story. Far too many experience a soured substitute of the Christian story and so dismiss it as irrelevant, outdated, or even harmful nonsense.

So if you can, try to look past what you have seen and heard from others, and pretend you are hearing the Christian story for the first time. For who knows? Perhaps in sampling the Christian story afresh, you might find that it tastes seriously good. Putting all our cards on the table as a disclaimer, this is our entire motivation for this book. There is nothing more natural to our humanity than wanting to share something we have come to love, so we wanted to tell you about a story that has changed our own lives, if only to give you the chance to consider it for yourself.

AN INVITATION TO REIMAGINE

One reason many people struggle to engage with the Christian story is because they don't quite understand how to approach the Bible. So much misunderstanding shrouds the true shape of this unique book. It is not a set of rules, though it does lay out a vision for what it means to live a full and meaningful life. Nor is the Bible a book of moral heroes, for all but one of the lives it details are deeply flawed, and we come face-to-face with the terrible fallout of their failures. Rather, the Bible is a sophisticated collection of ancient documents spanning a variety of genres that speak to life's deepest questions in often surprising ways. When pieced together, this library of books tells a unified story that stretches all the way back to our origins and points all the way forward into forever.

Our invitation is that you attempt to hear this story with fresh ears. Try to suspend disbelief long enough to consider whether or not the story sheds light on reality and matches the soulish contours of what you know, deep down, to be true. The first third of this book will simply spell out the arc of the Christian story through the six major scenes of the Bible, speaking to some of our culture's most pressing questions.[1] The second third of the book will explore what it would mean if you came to see that the story makes sense and you want to live out the script by stepping into a new or deeper relationship with God. The final third of the book will give voice to common questions and objections, allowing you to chase down thoughtful answers, and perhaps, in so doing, come to recognize that the Christian story is worth embracing.

PART ONE

THE CHRISTIAN STORY

Words and Flesh

*I believe in Christianity as I believe that the Sun has
risen, not only because I see it, but because by it
I see everything else.*

C. S. LEWIS
THE WEIGHT OF GLORY

Words have their limits. When we seek to explain love or
describe the feeling of wonder, even wordsmiths grasp
at something beyond reach. Language is simply too blunt a tool
for capturing the depths of reality, and nowhere is this more true
than when we speak about God. By definition God's inexhaust-
ible nature means finite creatures are only ever taking in a slice of
infinity, perhaps akin to the experience of trying to drink water
from a fire hydrant.

God simply transcends our total comprehension.

Even still, language can capture true things about God. Words
are how God has made Himself known. Creation was spoken
into being. Mathematics is the native tongue of our cosmos. Our
DNA spells out the longest word of biological information in the

known universe. You might say all of us are words. And these are all precursors to God speaking personally to humanity, condescending to make Himself known in history through our own languages and idioms.

The Christian story weaves together the distilled reflections of those who have seen the inexpressible with their eyes, touched the unexplainable with their hands, and felt their hearts strangely warmed by an indescribable presence. As the story develops over time, so does our ability to know what God is like, as we move from glimpsing God dimly through idioms and imagery to seeing God on full display as words take on flesh.

Our goal in feebly retelling the Christian story is not that you would be convinced by reason to believe in a distant concept, but that through the story, experiencing God's presence for yourself, you might be introduced to a real and living person: Jesus of Nazareth. We ourselves have met Jesus in the pages of the Bible, and we hope you too might be moved to reimagine the script you have adopted for your life, because Jesus invites you to step into something altogether better. So are you ready?

Let's begin.

ONE

The Garden: Created for Good

I would rather be what God chose to make me, than the most glorious creature that I could think of. For to have been thought about—born in God's thoughts—and then made by God, is the dearest, grandest, most precious thing in all thinking.

GEORGE MACDONALD
DAVID ELGINBROD

*So God created mankind in his own image,
in the image of God he created them;
male and female he created them.*

GENESIS 1:27

One of the curious features of the Christian story is that we are not the main characters.

The Bible does not begin with an account of human origins, nor even that of our cosmos. In the first book of the Bible, the opening words of Genesis claim that, before anything else existed, our Creator simply *was*. God is the prime subject as the Author of all reality, and the Scriptures are your invitation to know Him.*

The Bible teaches in its first sentence what Greek philosophers would only centuries later surmise—that prior to the inception of our universe, before the creation of everything out of nothing, beyond our space-time continuum, there had to be a first cause or prime mover from whom everything else that now exists finds its source.†

There is a quantum leap, though, between this god of the philosophers and the God of the Bible. For beyond a cold, rational hypothesis, the Bible reveals God in warm and relational terms. From beginning to end, we learn that our Creator is not only personal, but communal.

God is *Trinitarian.*

Now if you have never heard that word before (or even if you have), and find this idea strange or confusing, you are in noble company. The brightest Christian minds throughout the ages have marveled at this mystery, and some have even compared our attempt to make sense of the Trinity to a two-dimensional square grappling with descriptions of a three-dimensional cube.[2] Because in two dimensions, we are used to one square being one thing and another square being another thing entirely, we struggle to accept that somehow, in a higher dimension, six squares can also make up one thing. In this analogy, we humans are relatively

---

* Since this raises big questions, see Part 3: "Why Isn't God More Obvious?"
† Since this raises big questions, see Part 4: "Has Science Disproved God?"

simple creatures, more like the square, whereas God is more like a cube: a complex unity of one *what* (God) and three *who*'s (Father, Son, and Holy Spirit).

Before you throw down this book as too philosophical for your taste, the reason this matters so much to the storyline is, in a word, *love.* The idea that "God is love" is almost an axiom of modern spirituality, but God's nature cannot be relational or loving at the core if for eternity past God was *alone.* Love requires a personal connection between a subject, a *lover,* and an object, the *beloved.* So the notion of God as a Trinity opens up the possibility for love to find its source in the very nature of our Creator, for love has been eternally flowing from and to all three members of the Trinity.

And so it came to be that God's Trinitarian love sparked creation, in much the same way the loving union of a husband and wife tends to overflow into procreation. Beginning with the chaotic elements of creation, Genesis describes a process of developing order, where God brought about conditions conducive to life. A cosmically insignificant planet was granted incalculable dignity by becoming the epicenter of God's purposes. So earth began to teem with all manner of living things, filling the waterways, skies, and landscapes.

Amid the wild beauty of this new world, God cultivated a high garden to house humanity. Eden was a special place where heaven and earth overlapped, God's space and our space, where God's presence was even said to roam the gardens. As the crescendo of His creation, God imbued humanity with His divine image. Elected from among the earthly creatures, we were chosen to be like God, reflecting our Creator to the whole of creation.

This indelible imprint of God on each human soul is what gives everyone everywhere absolute status and worth, regardless of age, ability, gender, sexuality, race, religion, politics, or culture. Across history, this unique doctrine has served as an unassailable foundation for the universal dignity of all human beings, providing the soil out of which inalienable human rights can grow. And beyond what it has secured in horizontal or social terms, the vertical dimension of our special relationship to God speaks volumes into our earnest search for identity. For any journey to truly find ourselves must start by looking back to our origins.

One of life's inescapable questions is this: "*Who am I?*" From the first chapters of the Bible, from the opening scene of the Christian story, God's answer thunders back: we are God's earthly children, deeply loved, and masterfully created to be with and be like our heavenly Father.

When the reality of this identity dawns, it sheds light on all the meaningful things about who we are as human beings. Our hunger to love and be loved points back upstream to the headwaters of love itself, as we are made in the image of a relational God. Our consciousness and rationality are gifts of possessing a mind patterned after God's own mind, capable of unlocking the secrets God has woven into the universe. Our desires to create and contribute to culture are born out of our reflection of God's own creative drive and love of beauty. And our consciences are a window into the moral dimension of God's nature, serving as a compass to help us navigate right and wrong as the moral wisdom God has crafted into His creation.

So why did God create humans?

Here the second of life's inescapable questions is raised: "*Why am I here?*"

Genesis teaches that God created humans for deep and meaningful relationships and for a role. Humans were *created for good*: to love God, love each other, and cultivate the planet. Desiring that we would partner with Him as earthly children to a heavenly Father, God appointed humanity to continue bringing order from chaos as we spread our human communities around the planet. Humans were given the mandate to be the gardeners and governors of God's good world, taming a wild world beyond the borders of Eden as we build cultures, frame beauty, and foster the fruitfulness of the earth.

The entire shape of this creation is said to have brought God delight.

God's presence and God's world brought delight to our human hearts.

Eden was the *good life* because we were there with God.

TWO

The Tower: Damaged by Evil

*If only there were evil people somewhere insidiously
committing evil deeds, and it were necessary only to
separate them from the rest of us and destroy them.
But the line dividing good and evil cuts through the heart
of every human being.*

ALEKSANDR SOLZHENITSYN
THE GULAG ARCHIPELAGO

*The Lord saw how great the wickedness of the human
race had become on the earth.*

GENESIS 6:5

The garden scene just described is a far cry from the world we
now inhabit. Even though we still see glimpses of Eden in
who we are and what we want, this light to which we cling is often
eclipsed by a new shadow. Something sinister shrouds God's good
world, and you can hear its echo in our collective protest whenever

we stare evil and suffering in the face. This is not the way things should be. Something has gone wrong.

So what happened?

The second scene of the Christian story describes how although we were *created for good*, we have become *damaged by evil*. As moral creatures, designed for relationships and a role, humanity was faced with a choice, represented in Eden as a fruit tree. Either we could govern the world using God's wisdom, navigating life by trusting God's rule and definition of good and evil (a path God promises will lead to flourishing and freedom and life), or humans could redefine good and evil on their own terms, seizing power for themselves by eating the forbidden fruit (a path God warns will lead to a curse and captivity and death).

Why? Because any world of meaning is also a world of consequences. So to set the stage in this cosmic theater of meaning, God created a world where what we do greatly impacts us and our environment. Our choices matter. Cause and effect are built into the substructure of our universe. Not only does God govern matter and energy by upholding the regularity of what we call natural laws (a feature that enables us through science to harness nature for human enterprise), but God also wove a moral fabric into creation that governs the free actions of moral creatures (a feature that enables humans to live meaningful lives). Just like any attempt to break the laws of nature tends to end up with us being broken by them, God warned that to go against the moral grain of His design would always lead to suffering—only the symptoms of evil wouldn't stop with us. Since humans were appointed to be the gardeners and governors of God's world, if we were to walk off the job to pursue our own path, God knew the entire system would break down.

At this juncture in the Christian story, we are introduced to a dark and mysterious rebel, who aptly takes the form of a snake in order to spread a deadly poison. Known by many names (the devil, Satan, the enemy, the father of lies), this malevolent and shadowy creature tempts humanity to pursue life on their own terms, seeking to enlist them in his rebellion by deceiving them into breaking faith with God. And even though we had no reason to doubt God's goodness or doubt that His wisdom would lead to our flourishing and freedom and life, the snake's lies suggested there was something we were missing out on by trusting and obeying God.

What if God's moral design is more like a straitjacket than a path to freedom? What if God is holding us back from everything we could become? What if we can be happier as the authors of our own script?*

These temptations gave birth to the unthinkable: sin. A violation of our sacred purpose. Choosing to trust the snake, humanity exchanged the truth about God for a lie and traded the joy of eternal friendship with God for the thrill of a momentary and illicit pleasure.

The fallout from eating this forbidden fruit was catastrophic. Reaching for something more, we lost our true selves. While we were seeking to seize power, the power of evil seized us. What theologians describe as *the fall* is this space-time tragedy when human beings fell from their high calling as God's image-bearers

---

* Since this raises big questions, see Part 3: "What If The Snake Was Right?"

and crashed into the moral fabric of God's universe, whereby we and our world became *damaged by evil*.

Everything we knew about the good life with God began to unravel as the effects of our evil spread like a cancer throughout creation. A new specter of shame hung over us, such that we no longer felt safe being fully known and so rushed to hide behind fig leaves and fern bushes. As this erosion of intimacy led to a fracturing of our relationships, a deep sense of alienation set in. Where once the river of our desires was aimed at the good and innocence washed over our conscience like a cold spring, now these headwaters were polluted. Selfishness dethroned love in the human heart, curving us in on ourselves until all our desires were bent out of shape.

So where was God in this calamitous picture?

Never being caught by surprise, God's first reaction as He came to the garden was not explosive anger. Rather knowing all that we had done, like a loving parent, God called us out of hiding. The very first question out of God's mouth in the Bible paints the picture of Him earnestly seeking us out for relationship: "Where are you?" (Gen. 3:9)

With a broken heart from our rejection of His fatherly rule, God unfolded the tragic consequences of our rebellion. We would have to leave Eden. Sin would lead us into exile from the freedom and flourishing and life of God's presence.

Yet even while pronouncing this sentence, God comforts us with a promise of hope. Where we had failed to resist selfish desire and chaos, giving in to the temptation of a darker power, one day a new human will stand where we have fallen. In a showdown with evil, this Savior would be mortally wounded, yet through this pain would achieve a decisive victory and crush the snake's head.

Against the grim backdrop of the bad news of sin, this is the first glimpse of what Christians call the *gospel,* or the good news of the Christian story. Another closely follows. God substitutes our own attempts to cover up our shameful nakedness by clothing humanity in the skins of sacrificed animals. These twin prophetic acts, a promise and a provision, serve to foreshadow a coming hope. Someday, somewhere, somehow, God would send someone to save us from all we have done and become.

But that was still future. The hour had not yet come.

Even clothed in this hope, the exile from Eden was painful. The garden was where God had met with us personally. Eden was our taste of heaven on earth. But God's presence is dangerous for anyone *damaged by evil.* What theologians describe as God's holiness, the raw power of His unique presence, acts like a consuming fire. If you aren't made of the right stuff, then drawing near can be fatal. And so, because humanity were now corrupted by sin, for our own protection from His holy presence and to open the door for a plan of redemption, God sent us out into the wilderness beyond the borders of Eden. Only there, separated from God's life, we became vulnerable to sickness, suffering, and death. Where once in Eden the ground brought forth only good things, now in exile the fruitfulness of our work was frustrated, as the curse on creation brought forth thorns and thistles.

From here the scene grows dark. Sons and daughters were born in the wilderness, and the violence and injustice of a now-fallen humanity multiplied. With people redefining evil as good, everything sacred was trampled. Brother killed brother. Men enslaved women. Tools of war became a trade. The human heart hardened. As we pursued darker powers, trading God's benevolent rule for the tyrannical reign of diabolical gods and human dictators, our descent from Eden into evil accelerated.*

Eventually humanity unites under a murderous ruler to reach a second time for something more. Convinced that our earthly achievements could give us a sense of permanence and significance and satisfaction, humans constructed a corrupt civilization in Babel (Babylon). At the heart of this evil empire was a tower, a structure to help us reach back into the heavens—a misguided quest to remake Eden on our own terms.

It was an attempt to create the good life without God as King.

But Babylon always fails to deliver on its promises. Because we were made for God's presence, nothing and no one else can fill the void left by God's absence. All attempts to put something or someone in God's place only ends up disappointing us and hurting others. Since God knew that concentrating evil in a single empire would be disastrous for the human project and His plan of redemption, He intervened. Aware that words build worlds, God came down to confuse our tongues, such that the proliferation of new languages led to a scattering of tribes and an abandonment of Babylon.

At least for a time.

These first two scenes of the Christian story shed remarkable light on our human experience. That we were *created for good*

---

* Since this raises big questions, see Part 3: "How Could a Good God Allow Suffering?"

explains everything deep and beautiful and rich about who we are and that we have become *damaged by evil* makes sense of the darkness, distance, and death we all experience and see within our own hearts. Something has gone wrong: evil. Only this dark power is not something outside of us we can simply push or wish away, for there exists within all of us a war between the divine and the diabolical.

We are now a mixture of Eden and evil.

We live in the shadow of exile.

The Nation: Chosen to Bless

If the statistics are right, the Jews constitute but one quarter of one percent of the human race. It suggests a nebulous puff of star dust lost in the blaze of the Milky Way. Properly, the Jew ought hardly to be heard of, but he is heard of, has always been heard of. He is as prominent on the planet as any other people, and his importance is extravagantly out of proportion to the smallness of his bulk.

MARK TWAIN
"CONCERNING THE JEWS"

"I will also make you a light for the Gentiles, that my salvation may reach to the ends of the earth."

ISAIAH 49:6

With the close of the last scene focused on the scattering of fallen humanity away from Babylon, the third scene of the Christian story begins with God gathering a new people for a new purpose in a new land. With a paradoxical wisdom so typical of God, His cosmic plan to rescue the whole world from sin and death begins by breathing new life into an unsuspecting and unspectacular family.

God elected an elderly barren couple, Abraham and Sarah, and invited them to leave behind everything familiar to join Him on a new adventure of faith. And here God intervened to bring about a miracle baby for the first time in the Christian story (though certainly not the last). God's promise to this new family was that they would multiply to become a great nation, Israel, set apart to show the rest of the world the way back to the good life with God.

Israel was a nation *chosen to bless.*

Over a small number of generations passing through Abraham, Isaac, and Jacob, it seemed as though all God's promises were coming true. What began with a humble couple grew into a huge family of twelve tribes. But then a few generations later, with fortunes radically changed, Israel found themselves enslaved in Egypt.

The dramatic exodus of Israel from Egypt serves as a paradigm in the Christian story of God delivering His people from the powers that hold them captive. The people of Israel were set free to live free, which is still the pattern of all who encounter God. Led by Moses, Israel's miraculous escape from Pharaoh's forces was followed closely by the people's special encounter with God at the foot of Mt. Sinai, where God bound Himself to this young nation in a renewed covenant. In this sacred agreement, God promised that His presence would dwell among His people in a tent or a temple. In return, Israel committed to following Torah, God's law, as the way for them to draw near to God's holy presence in safety, and to reflect God's goodness to the surrounding nations as a light in a world of shadows.

Torah laid out a total way of life. The 613 commands represented God's ethical vision for navigating an ancient community toward the good life: God's desire for justice through welfare and charity; God's holy character through the ritual laws; and God's provision for sin through the priestly and sacrificial systems. The religious calendar of sabbaths (rest days), feasts, and festivals recounted the shape of Israel's story, reminding them of who they were, why they existed, and what God had done for them.

Even still, Torah was not the endgame. God's holy presence was never intended to be confined to a temple, separated from His people by a veil. The entire system pointed forward in preparation for the coming of a new way. One day the Messiah would come to fulfill the purposes of Torah, break the spell of evil, and tear open the veil in order to re-establish God's good rule and holy presence throughout all of creation.

But that too was still future. The hour had not yet come.

As God brought Israel into the promised land, a new garden paradise from which the former tenants had been exiled for evil, Torah represented the same choice Adam and Eve had been given in the garden. Would Israel govern their lives according to God's wise rule as king, trusting God that the way of Torah would lead to their freedom and flourishing and life, or would they break faith and walk away from their covenant with God, doing what was right in their own eyes?

Tragically the story did not go well. Rather than living for love of God and neighbor, Israel chased after false gods as a means of hoarding blessings for themselves. Rather than bearing witness to the surrounding nations by trusting God as their king, Israel sought to become like other nations by appointing a human ruler.

Even though Israel rejected God's kingly rule, He continued to love them and even used the new office of a human king as a vehicle to serve His purposes. For where all of Israel's kings failed to live up to Torah, the prophecy arose that one day an anointed king would arise to establish God's kingdom on earth. God promised King David, a moral mess with a soft heart for God, that one of his descendants would be the Messiah, ushering in an eternal age of God's peace, justice, and prosperity.

But that too was still future. The hour had not yet come.

Over time the Israelite people went through cycles of neglecting Torah, splintering into factions, and descending into ruin, only to be saved periodically by God's faithfulness. As a betrayed lover, God kept stepping in to rescue His people, His adulterous bride. Any bright moments of revival in the aftermath of God's grace were short-lived, scattered amid longer periods of darkness when Israel followed after corrupt leaders. Rather than setting themselves apart from the pagan religious worship of other nations in order to light the way to God, Israel became consumed by the same dark pursuits. Evil's grip on the human heart seemed so thorough that even Israel's wisest kings would often succumb to the snake's temptations, chase their own desires, and turn their back on Torah.

Israel cheated on God so much that they failed in their purpose.

After being warned for generations that sin would once again lead to exile, eventually Babylon came. Led by a new murderous ruler, Babylon's violent armies swallowed up God's city of peace. Jerusalem fell. And ascending to the elevated mountaintop where Israel met with their Creator, Babylon tore down the temple as the house of God's holy presence. This was an unbearably traumatic and disorienting experience.

Israel had to come to terms with their failure as they were carried off into exile as captives. Even with God's special guidance, even with Torah, even with living in the shade of God's Temple, they found themselves again in the dark shadow of Babel's tower. Their hardness of heart made Torah impossible, such that they could not live up to who they were chosen to be.

So what hope remained?

The rest of Israel's story in the Jewish Scriptures comes from a strange band of people on the margins of society known as prophets. These were people who spoke for God, calling Israel forward in faithfulness to the goodness and justice and truth of God's way. As Israel eventually returned from Babylon to start the process of rebuilding, these prophets foretold a future when God's presence would come in a new way through a new leader. As Israel awaited a new exodus to free their hearts from captivity to evil, they looked forward to a messianic king who could resist the snake's temptations when every other human had failed. Someone sent from God to embody the light of Torah. Someone who could cover over all of their failures. Someone who could transform hard hearts so we can make the right choice. Someone who could lead everyone back to the good life with God.

And with these scattered whispers of a coming Messiah, the part of the Christian story known as the Old Testament comes to an end, and we are left with the following questions.

Does God still care about the suffering of our world?

How will God deal with the evil that holds us captive?

Are we still loved despite all we have done?

An Interlude
(Selah)

As the Old Testament closes and leaves open a series of questions, the New Testament opens with Jesus as God's answer. Like an author writing themselves into the script, eternal Spirit becomes physical matter as our Creator enters His creation. The scandalous claim of the Christian story is that Jesus is the invisible God made visible.

This claim to be God is one no other religious luminary before or since has made! Perhaps those suffering from a delusion, sure, but none who have become widely believed. For Jesus to stake His reputation on His claim to be God means He shut the door to us simply taking Him as a wise sage, moral teacher, or religious prophet. Of course the claim that a finite human being could somehow also be the infinite God is a difficult pill for anyone to swallow. No self-respecting first-century Jew, let alone a skeptically-minded person of our time, would accept that claim without demanding some seriously compelling evidence. But that is precisely the point.

Everything hinges on the evidence.

Perhaps one of the most unique and striking elements of the Christian story is that it is not merely religious philosophy or ideology, for its central claims are based on historical events that can be investigate and verified. That Jesus is history is what makes the gospel *good news* rather than simply a *good idea*. Christians believe that the One who made the world has left His historical footprint on it. And just like the first eyewitnesses, you are invited to investigate His claims, starting with the carefully preserved stories that make up our New Testament sources.* To these we now turn for the final three scenes of the Christian story.

---

* Since this raises big questions, see Part 3: "Can I Trust the Bible?"

FOUR

The Cross: Redeemed by Love

As a child I received instruction both in the Bible and in the Talmud. I am a Jew, but I am enthralled by the luminous figure of the Nazarene. . . . No one can read the gospels without feeling the actual presence of Jesus. His personality pulsates in every word. No myth is filled with such life. . . . Jesus is too colossal for the pen of phrase mongers, however artful.

ALBERT EINSTEIN
"WHAT LIFE MEANS TO EINSTEIN," *SATURDAY EVENING POST*

The Word became flesh and made his dwelling among us. We have seen his glory, the glory of the one and only Son, who came from the Father, full of grace and truth.

JOHN 1:14

I n the fourth scene of the Christian story, Jesus of Nazareth comes that we might be *redeemed by love*. The New Testament opens with the prophesied arrival of another miracle baby, only this time, he wasn't born from a barren womb but a virgin one. Having the supernatural power to create everything out of nothing at the inception of our universe, God caused a miraculous conception that led, nine months later, to the virgin birth of Jesus. God set this miracle against the backdrop of the regularity of nature to send us a clear message.

Someone special had arrived on earth.

God had come to make Himself known.

What we now celebrate as the Christmas story fulfills ancient predictions dating all the way back to the garden of Eden. The little feet of the baby Jesus so familiar to us from nativity scenes are the same ones destined to one day crush the snake's head. God's timeless plan to save us from sin and death was ramping up toward fulfilment.

But how?

The answer to this question unfolds across the Gospels.

While the reports of Jesus' early life are scarce, it seems for the first three decades He lived a humble existence working in the trade of His adoptive father, Joseph. The God-man spent His days and nights dignifying everyday work by shaping the raw materials of creation to make them useful for human enterprise. Yet when the time had finally come, His focus shifted, and Jesus joined His heavenly Father to work on a new creation.

When Jesus was about thirty years old, He shed anonymity and went public. Having never sinned, and with nothing of which he needed to repent, Jesus identified with our human story and Israel's struggle by embracing a baptism of repentance through his cousin, John the Baptizer. He had come to be our new human representative, and heaven wanted us to know. As Jesus emerged from the river after His baptism, the sky broke open, God the Father declared His love for Jesus the Son, and the Holy Spirit descended upon Jesus like a dove. Just as creation was the overflow of Trinitarian love, so too does the Trinity take center stage to launch the work of new creation.

The hour long promised had finally arrived.

After a brief episode in the wilderness as His first showdown with the snake, Jesus launched a public ministry of teaching and miracles. Across His travels Jesus went to war with the symptoms and forces of evil, as He was stirred by compassion for friend and foe alike. Jesus healed the sick wherever He went, restoring beauty to the blind, music to the deaf, and dancing to the lame. With a single lunchbox, Jesus fed a whole stadium, and He transformed barrels of water into vintage wine, all the while promising that only He could satisfy our deepest hungers and thirsts. Such was the reach of His miraculous power that Jesus left footprints on the sea, and the elements of creation, the wind and the waves, responded on command at the call of their Creator. On a few occasions, when it seemed as though all hope was snuffed out, Jesus simply plundered the grave, reaching down into death to pull loved ones back to life. And when people were tormented by malevolence, captive to demons, and deemed a lost cause, Jesus' mere presence spelled freedom as evil fled in fear. These sorts of signs were Jesus' new trademark, slowly awakening His followers to the true identity of who they were following.

Everywhere He went, Jesus preached about the coming king-dom of God and how to live now as though God had once again become king. To a world divided by rampant tribalism, Jesus said to love our enemies and pray for our persecutors. To a culture full of hypocritical performers, Jesus said we should humbly seek God in secret. To a people who sought earthly power and position, Jesus said that true greatness means not to be served but to serve, stooping down to embrace the humblest station. He taught that humans should steer from violence, flee from temptation, and give without thought of measure. And when Jesus spoke, His words carried an inscrutable wisdom and unparalleled authority, such that His critics were silenced and the crowds were awestruck.

Jesus' sublime teaching was matched only by the singular caliber of His life. He put flesh on His words, living His whole existence as one continuous sermon. Each encounter recorded in the Gospels serves as a muse to imagine how different the world would be if we followed God's wisdom and were animated by God's presence. To the bewilderment of the elite and the establishment, Jesus flipped the social ladder by embracing the ostracized, marginalized, and forgotten. He validated the voices and vocation of women and dignified children by holding them up as examples. With a moral genius never before seen, somehow the holiest man who ever lived, without giving an inch toward evil, became a magnet for criminals, sinners, and outcasts. Anyone who had been written off as damaged goods, or not eligible for social standing, seemed a prime candidate for Jesus' motley crew of disciples. Wherever the letter of the law had been abused to shut people out, Jesus, as the author and spirit of the law, tore down the walls.

What is so enigmatic about Jesus is how soft He was toward sinners, even though He never soft-pedaled sin. He lived up to the prophecy made about Him, that a bruised reed He would not break and a smoldering wick He would not snuff out. Still, His central message represented a profound challenge: *Repent.* Give up any allegiance to the snake and to sin and realign with the dawning reality where God again is king. For those who knew firsthand the bitter aftertaste of sin, Jesus' invitation was irresistible.

Just as the Jesus movement was picking up steam and all Israel was looking for a military Messiah to overthrow their Roman overlords, Jesus chose a different path. For as He had been teaching His disciples, our true enemy was not another human tribe *out there,* but rather unseen sinister forces and a dark power *inside.* Any corrupt human systems are only ever an outward embodiment of this inward disorder. Israel's deeper captivity was not to the Roman Empire as a new kind of Babylon but to the snake and to sin. The same has been true of all of us, ever since our hearts became *damaged by evil.* As the grand physician of our souls, Jesus diagnosed that we all have a spiritual sickness that exiles us from God's holy presence. This condition is tragically terminal, leading to death and judgment thereafter.

So how can Jesus save us?

Before God created a single atom, He knew the terrible price to be paid in order to deal with evil. Forgiveness is never free; someone always absorbs the cost. The Christian story says that the *cross of Christ* was not a mere accident of history, but an intentional act of atonement. When God used the skins of dead animals to cover over the shame of Adam and Eve, or when He prescribed sacrifices for sin as part of Torah, these were merely signposts pointing toward an ultimate sacrifice where Jesus would trade His perfect life to cover over our evil.

This is where Jesus continually faced His own temptation. The cross serves as Torah did for Israel and the tree did in Eden. It represents Jesus' choice: either Jesus can trust His Father's love and endure the cross to save us, or He can go off script and save Himself. Astoundingly, for the first time in the Christian story, someone stood up to the snake's temptation. Whether after His baptism in the wilderness or when His followers pleaded with Jesus to avoid the cross, or when in Gethsemane's garden His spirit felt the anguish of His impending death, Jesus never for a moment doubted God or succumbed to the snake. Jesus succeeded where all other humans had failed. After sharing a special meal with His followers, Jesus allowed Himself to be arrested, laying down His life of His own accord, and endured for our sake all that was about to come.

The next twenty-four hours were a travesty of justice. The religious authorities conspired to have Jesus executed on trumped-up charges that were never substantiated. A series of six trials were painful and shameful, conducted either under a shroud of secrecy or amid the screams of a frenzied mob. Jesus was beaten mercilessly, stripped down, and spat upon before being pulverized by a brutal lashing that stripped flesh from the bone. Then to satisfy the sadistic whims of the guards, thorns were pressed into Jesus' skull and His wounds were mockingly covered by a scarlet robe. Laughing off His claim to be king, the soldiers unwittingly dramatized the true meaning of Jesus' death, crowning Him with our curse and shrouding Him with our sin.

To satisfy the murderous demands of the crowds, the Roman governor, Pontius Pilate, who could find no fault in Jesus, still sentenced Him to a criminal's death. Jesus was made to carry His own heavy cross to a lonely hill outside the walls of Jerusalem, Golgotha. There He endured the most excruciating death the Roman war machine could mastermind. Jesus was crucified, with large spikes nailed through the nerve clusters of His wrists and ankles. The sky grew dark as creation mourned its Maker's suffering, yet even as His blood soaked the earth below, what came out of Jesus was nothing short of divine love: prayers for His executioners, provision for His mother, and promises to a thief. After hours of agony as His strength ebbed away, the One who breathed life into our nostrils had that breath leave His own.

That moment triggered a profound reaction. The earth shook. Graves were opened. The veil cloistering God's holy presence in the Temple was torn asunder. What was happening? When with His dying breaths Jesus declared, *Tetelestai*, translated, *it is finished*, the *it* was His work of atonement. Everything that was necessary for sinners to come close to a holy God was completed at the cross. Evil's power to exile us from God had been exhausted, and the apocalyptic symbols surrounding Jesus' death played out that breathtaking drama.

Earth was cracking open, and heaven came flooding through.

The Cross of Christ is the clearest window we have in the Christian story into the holy love of God. There we encounter a God who cares so much about evil, and what it has done to damage us and distort His creation, that He cannot justly leave it unpunished. At the same time we encounter a God who loves us so much that He would rather step in to absorb that punishment than see us endure it. The Cross simultaneously exposes all we have become and all God is willing to suffer so we can be *redeemed by love.*

Once Jesus was pronounced dead by His executioners, His corpse was taken down and buried in a sealed tomb. One might have expected the Christian story to end there, as simply another in a long list of failed Jewish messianic movements quashed by the might of Rome. Jesus of Nazareth should be nothing more than a footnote on a judicial register in a small and insignificant province of the ancient world.

But something remarkable changed the course of history.

When Jesus was alive, He foretold that His burial would not sound the drum of defeat. Rather, any brief interlude in which He was swallowed up by the grave would be heaven's reckoning with darkness and death. And death would prove no match for the Author of life.

After three days in the ground came the dawn of Easter Sunday, and with it Jesus opened His eyes and breathed deeply of new creation. God supernaturally raised Jesus from the dead, a miracle that not only certified Jesus' divine claim but also opened the door to a whole new reality.* For if Jesus overcame the grave, demoting death from a full-stop to a comma in the sentence of reality, then we can trust His promise that eternal life belongs to whoever believes in Him.

Over a period of forty days, hundreds of people became eye-witnesses to Jesus' resurrection. Jesus ate with them, entertained their doubts, and answered their questions. And just as they

————————

* Since this raises big questions, see Part 3: "Did Jesus Really Rise from the Dead?"

sought to hold onto Him, Jesus announced it was time for Him to leave. The first phase of His mission on earth had come to an end. A new way had been opened for all the nations of the earth to be blessed through Israel. All they needed to do to step into God's story and find eternal life was to believe in Israel's Messiah.

They could give up writing their own script and receive the Cross.

But who would be the ones to tell them?

FIVE

The Church: Sent Together to Heal

Just as a weak flame is blown out easily by a small breeze, so a weak faith . . . may be extinguished quickly when it encounters evil and suffering. But real faith is more like a strong flame—a storm only fans it into an inextinguishable blaze.

OS GUINNESS
UNSPEAKABLE

They devoted themselves to the apostles' teaching and to fellowship, to the breaking of bread and to prayer. Everyone was filled with awe at the many wonders and signs performed by the apostles. All the believers were together and had everything in common. They sold property and possessions to give to anyone who had need.

ACTS 2:42–45

The fifth scene of the Christian story centers around the emergence of something called *the church.* The Gospel stories close with Jesus gathering His closest friends and followers, some still full of doubts, to give them His last standing orders. They would be the ones to take the *breaking news* of Jesus' death and resurrection to the rest of the world. Against all odds and opposition, their task was to embody Jesus' legacy and spread the Christian story, so that whoever believes could step into a new or deeper relationship with God. Like with Abraham, this great commission was to leave everything familiar and set out on an adventure of faith, so God could gather to Himself a new people comprised of every tribe and tongue from all across the earth.

That is the mission of the church: Christians were *sent together to heal.*

But how?

What can transform ordinary people to follow Jesus' way of the Cross?

Before Jesus ascended into heaven, He told His followers to wait in Jerusalem. Jesus was going away so another helper could come. The Holy Spirit. God's personal presence and power. Ten days later, something remarkable happened. While the disciples were gathered together in a locked room on the day of Pentecost (one of the Jewish festivals), the fire of God's presence filled the air and flooded their hearts. Jesus' followers sensed something changing. God was making them new from the inside out. The Holy Spirit had sparked a spiritual rebirth, enabling them to say no to the snake's temptations and embrace the way of the Cross. What the fall had disordered when we became *damaged by evil,* the Holy Spirit was beginning to set right.

And so it happened that a movement unlike any other in the history of the world was born. This moment marked the birth of the church, where God's holy presence was no longer cloistered in tents or temples built by human hands. Now He dwelled *in* His people. Christians became mobile temples, taking God's presence with them wherever they went as hotspots of heaven on earth. And God's power animated them to do the impossible.

Where God had scattered humanity by confusing their languages at Babel, now at Pentecost He began a global gathering of tribes and tongues by enabling Jesus' followers to tell the Christian story in languages they never knew. Pilgrims from all over the world who had traveled to Jerusalem for the festival were able to hear these Christians talking about Jesus in their own native tongue. This supernatural spectacle led to the explosion of the church as three thousand believed and were baptized in a single day. From now on, the church would be unstoppable, though that didn't stop some from trying.

The religious and political establishments were furious that people continued to follow Jesus after they had gone to such great lengths to put Him down forever. And that the Jesus movement endured was made all the more offensive by the fact that these Christians were now openly worshiping Jesus as Lord. Chief among the opposition was a man named Saul of Tarsus, who went out of his way to stamp out the Jesus movement. Taking to violence under the guise of religious zeal, Saul approved of the stoning of Stephen, the first Christian martyr, and, having driven the church underground, sought to smoke out Christians from wherever they were hiding.

One day, though, Saul had a dramatic encounter on the road to Damascus that forever changed him. He had a special encounter with the resurrected Jesus. This radical conversion to believing in Jesus catapulted Saul from being the chief persecutor of Christians to becoming the greatest advocate for the Christian story in the ancient world. Perhaps now better known as the apostle Paul, he was the one to translate the Christian story across new cultural barriers. From Jerusalem to Rome, Paul powerfully made the case for Christianity right up until the day he was beheaded for preaching the gospel, with new opponents approving of his death.

Nowhere did Jesus promise that the way of the Cross would be easy, nor is the church a perfect beacon lighting the path to life with God. Far from it. Every letter in the New Testament was written to encourage endurance through difficult times or because something in the beliefs or behaviors of the early Jesus movement came up short, sometimes drastically so, and needed to be corrected.* Because love is still God's goal or endgame, freedom is still God's means, leaving open the door for Christians, like the rest of the human race, to forget the way of the Cross and wander off script.

The church exists for something beautiful. To be the epicenter of God's work in the world. The hands and feet of God's love. The carriers of the Christian story. Those who together bear witness to the legacy of Jesus, opposing evil and inviting people everywhere to step into a new or deeper relationship with God through faith in the death and resurrection of Jesus.

That is, of course, until Jesus comes again.

But what will that be like?

---

* Since this raises big questions, see Part 3: "How Can God Be Good When the Church Is So Bad?"

SIX

The City:
Set Everything Right

Darkness cannot drive out darkness,
only light can do that.

MARTIN LUTHER KING JR.
STRENGTH TO LOVE

"'He will wipe every tear from their eyes. There will be
no more death' or mourning or crying or pain, for the old
order of things has passed away."

REVELATION 21:4

The final scene of the Christian story spells out our destiny, where Jesus comes back to *set everything right*. Rarely will you find people who do not long in their bones for justice. For wrongs to be set right. For those who have done evil to stand trial. For the oppressed to be set free. For light to chase away all of the shadows of darkness.

Scattered throughout the New Testament is the sure expectation that one day Jesus will return to weed out evil and exile it from God's future world. As the cosmic Judge, Jesus is tasked with executing judgment, restoring justice, and ushering in the kingdom of God in the new heavens and new earth. He comes to wash away the effects of the curse on creation and wipe away the tears of all who are willing to come to Him. That restoration is God's desire for everyone, and only two things stop us from entering this reality.

Our records and our hearts.

First, our records. As much as we might rejoice at the notion of a world without evil, we often forget there is a flip side to this justice equation. We tend to be passionate about justice when other people have done wrong, but we shy away from it when our own deeds are under review. In the grand scheme of things, as people *damaged by evil,* we are both the perpetrators and the victims. Considered against the backdrop of who we were created to be, none of us come close to living up to the mark. All of us are guilty.

The last pages of the Bible, along with scattered references throughout, describe in symbolic language what this judgment scene will be like. Jesus is set to return like a thief in the night, when the world least expects His coming. Then everyone who has ever lived will be resurrected to face final judgment. There the great ledgers will be opened, revealing our good works but also exposing our every evil thought, word, and deed, along with all the good things we left undone. When dealing with perfect justice there are no deals to be struck, such that anyone who tries to stand on their record will find the ground fall out beneath them.

Second, our hearts. Evil cannot enter God's new creation. Even if our record was wiped clean and our ledgers emptied, our hearts, still captive to evil, would corrupt the world all over again. Even more, the thing that makes God's future world a paradise, what makes the Christian vision of eternity unique, is that our happiness doesn't flow from an endless assortment of physical pleasures. We are made eternally happy because *God* is there with us. Whereas in Eden's garden God came down to walk with humanity, our future is to experience God's permanent presence in a glorious new city.

One could describe the grand narrative of the Bible as a love story between heaven and earth, with eternity ushering in a cosmic marriage where the two once-separate spaces finally come together. There and then, the intensity of God's holy presence will so permeate creation that His light is set to replace the sun, and in the same way a fiery forge can either purify or destroy, our experience of God's presence changes depending on the state of our hearts. The new heavens and new earth would be hellish for any whose hearts are still *damaged by evil.*

The existence of an alternative to eternity with God is a heavy reality. Across the Christian story, this place goes by many descriptions: *outer darkness, the lake of fire,* or *the second death.* And while the Bible is vague on the details, what we do know is that to write your own script ends in tragedy. There the tale of two cities ends as Babylon is forever destroyed. And anyone who chooses to hold on to evil rather than cling to Jesus must face exile one final time; only, from this separation, there is no return. Everything that corrupts creation must be removed, and to be cut off from the eternal life and love of God is an unthinkable loss compared to what is on offer.

Jesus paid a crimson currency to free us from such a fate. And so, in the judgment scene, we have another book opened, the Book of Life, which records the names of all who have trusted in Jesus. Together they have traded their guilty record for the singularly righteous ledger of Jesus' life. And rather than come to the gates of eternity with a heart *damaged by evil*, at our resurrection, everything subhuman will have fallen away. We are promised to be awakened with immortal bodies made ready for the paradise of God's holy presence. There we are set to work again, ruling and reigning with Jesus, as the gardeners and governors of the new creation.

With this scene, the Christian story comes to a close with a yearning for Jesus' return, as He will bring with Him the flourishing and freedom and life of the new creation. Our eternal destiny, and the entire shape of our lives here, hinges on how we respond to the Christian story and what we do with Jesus' invitation to believe in and follow Him.

To those who want lives permeated by meaning,

Jesus beckons *come.*

To those whose hungers have gone unsatisfied,

Jesus beckons *come.*

To those who feel weighed down by failure,

Jesus beckons *come.*

To those who seek life and immortality,

Jesus beckons *come.*

To those who long to drink deep of love,

Jesus beckons *come.*

Perhaps you still have questions before being able to answer Jesus' invitation, which is why Part 3 of this book seeks to offer some thoughtful answers to common objections. If that's where you are on the journey, peruse those questions and answers now. Perhaps, though, like untold billions before you, you're ready to consider Jesus' invitation to believe in and follow Him. If that is where you are on the journey of faith, then read on into Part 2 to see what it might look like for you to step into God's story.

PART TWO

STEPPING INTO
THE STORY

A Personal Invitation

The Christian ideal has not been tried and found wanting.
It has been found difficult; and left untried.

G. K. CHESTERTON
WHAT'S WRONG WITH THE WORLD

"Come, follow me."

MATTHEW 4:19

J esus extends to you a personal invitation. That is the source of why, for two millennia now, the Jesus movement has never stopped expanding across borders and into new tribes and tongues. Jesus comes to each of us, and the invitation has always been personal.

Just like He did with His first disciples, Jesus invites you by name to believe in and follow Him. You are now part of the long line of history, as people of every generation have had to decide for themselves whether to answer or ignore Jesus' call.

But what exactly is the nature of that invitation?

What does it mean to become a Christian?

Across the ages, this moniker *Christian* has collected all sorts of cultural baggage so that Christianity can seem nebulous, confusing people of all persuasions (not least of all Christians). Some people think being a Christian is primarily about subscribing to the right set of beliefs, collecting a certain set of spiritual experiences, or devotion to a particular catalog of religious rituals and ethics. Right thinking, right feeling, or right doing. While being a Christian cannot be divorced from our beliefs and behaviors, any mechanistic description like this is an inadequate frame.

As we look back through time, we discover that the label *Christian* was likely a derogatory tag for the emerging Jesus movement. Whereas this community tended to self-identify as *followers of the Way*, it was their detractors who called them *Christians* (meaning *little Christs*). But rather than being embarrassed by the slander, the first Christians adopted that label as a badge of honor as they aspired to follow in the footsteps of Jesus.

Perhaps the best way, though, to come at defining Christianity is to let the Bible shape our answer. As best we can distill, becoming a Christian is fundamentally about stepping into the Christian story in response to Jesus' invitation to believe in Him and follow Him. And first and foremost that means beginning *a new relationship* with God.

This is the beating heart of the Jesus movement.

From here, a new life story begins to emerge as we embrace *a new community* gathered around the gospel, receive from God *a new identity* as our foundation for self-understanding and expression, follow Jesus' roadmap into *a new way to live*, and launch into *a new purpose* for our lives. No doubt this is all a lot to take in, as is always true of any worthy adventure. After all, stepping into the Christian story brings you into a whole new reality, as every priority in life is reframed by God's Spirit and script.

We would be remiss, though, if we failed to warn that the road ahead is hard. Wisdom dictates that you should know what you are in for before you respond to Jesus' invitation. Even Jesus often challenged His closest friends and followers to count the cost, many of whom faced immense hardship in life and even suffered imprisonment or execution for going public about their belief in Jesus. To differing degrees for each of us, depending who we are and where we live, the choice to believe in and follow Jesus will mean serious sacrifices. And while we cannot always know in advance what that will be, this much is clear: Christianity is not a path one should traverse if you are looking for comfort or convenience; for although with one hand Jesus invites all who are weary and burdened to come to Him for rest, with the other, He hands you a cross and bids you to die to your own selfish desires. What catapulted the first Christians into embracing this cost is that they had met Jesus, and in their estimation, He was worth giving everything for. Only here is the paradoxical kicker: death to self turned out to be a doorway into a joy they never imagined.

So in this second part of the book, we will try to map out in summary detail what it means to step into the Christian story and why, despite the foreseeable and unseen costs, we think the invitation of Jesus is worth embracing. Each of the five new realities we outline will come with a brief explanation from the Christian story along with a few practical steps you can take if, at the end, you decide you want to personally step into the story. As something of a bonus, finally, we'll recommend resources to help you dive deeper.

ONE

A New Relationship

To all who did receive him, to those who believed in his name, he gave the right to become children of God.

JOHN 1:12

We take our very first step into the Christian story by beginning a new relationship with God. The Bible describes God neither as an impersonal force nor as a generic concept or theory but as a loving heavenly Father who is searching us out for relationship.

Now this idea might be difficult, perhaps even painful for some of us, for our frame of reference when it comes to earthly father figures can too easily be tainted. What if I am known but rejected? What if I open up only to be let down? But God sees you. He cares about your story. And God doesn't pretend we don't carry scars from our past; but as proof that we can trust Him, for all eternity, God the Son now bears scars of His own.

According to the Christian story, although we were *created for good* to know and be known by God, because we became *damaged by evil*, we were all at one time alienated from God. No one is born a Christian. The scandalous claim of the gospel is that even knowing us to the depths, warts and all, a holy God still loves us so unreservedly that He was willing to endure the cross to purchase our freedom. By virtue of His grace, and His grace alone, Jesus absorbed all the shame and suffering our sin incurred, embracing death in order that our estrangement might end and we might be ushered home.

Jesus' death and resurrection mean our relationship status with God can be changed. Through faith in Him, we can be born again into God's family. There we are welcomed with open arms to experience Trinitarian love with a new heavenly Father, Jesus as our elder brother, and the Holy Spirit making God's home in us. At God's table, we are fully known and profoundly loved, regardless of our failings. No longer is there any need to filter our tumultuous inner life, for now we can run to Him instinctively, just as a child runs without inhibition to the warmth of a loving parent's embrace. As cosmic as the scope of God's love may be, He is intimately interested in us, personally and specifically. Unlike earthly parents whose time and emotional resources have limits, the infinite ocean of God's love has no boundaries and so cannot be exhausted.

Having a relationship with God is, in some ways, like having a relationship with anyone else. To grow closer, we have to spend time together and share the deepest parts of ourselves. God's personal presence is not something we must beg for or pretend about but a beautiful reality to which we can become increasingly aware over time.

This is why for thousands of years Christians have practiced simple disciplines modeled by Jesus to draw closer to God. To speak with our heavenly Father in prayer, to read and meditate on what the Bible teaches about God, to praise Him and engage our deepest emotions through hymns and songs, to experience wonder and express awe by spending time in God's creation, and to spend time with the rest of God's family, experiencing Him through the lives and words of others.

There are near-endless variations and traditions within these disciplines, but they all share the goal of deepening our relationship with God and transforming who we are. Were you to choose to take up Jesus' invitation to step into the Christian story, here are some first steps you can take to grow in your relationship with God.

STEPPING IN:
BEGINNING A NEW RELATIONSHIP

Discover

Perhaps the best way to grow any relationship is to discover more about the other person. Although we can learn about God in many ways, Jesus says, "Anyone who has seen me has seen the Father" (John 14:9). So the character of Jesus is the full and perfect revelation of the character of God. Therefore reading the accounts of Jesus' life (in Matthew, Mark, Luke, and John) is a great place to start discovering *who* God is.

- **Choose** a way to read/listen to the Bible (see resources given below).
- **Learn** about the context of what you are reading (Who? What? When? Where? Why?).
- **Imagine** yourself as one of the characters. Ask, what would it have felt like to be in their shoes? How would I have responded? What does this teach me about God, myself, and the gospel? How should I respond to this part of the Bible?
- **Go slow.** There is no need to rush. Work through your assumptions and feelings, and ask the Holy Spirit to speak to you.
- **Write** down questions that come up from the story/ passage. Ask someone who knows the Bible well to help you find answers.
- **Carve** out a daily time to keep discovering more about God.

Connect

Like any other relationship, growing in your relationship with God requires time spent together. Prayer is a way of communicating meaningfully with God and sharing our lives with Him. When Jesus' disciples asked Him to teach them how to pray, He taught them to speak frequently, privately, simply, and honestly. He taught them the follow- ing model, commonly known as the *Lord's Prayer*:

"Our Father in heaven,
hallowed be your name,

your kingdom come,

your will be done,

   on earth as it is in heaven.

Give us today our daily bread.

And forgive us our debts,

   as we also have forgiven our debtors.

And lead us not into temptation,

   but deliver us from the evil one."

One memorable approach to communicating with God is spelled out P-R-A-Y.[3]

- **P**ause: Prayer starts by stopping. Take a moment to be still and fully present with God.
- **R**ejoice: Take time to acknowledge the beauty and wonder of God and worship Him.
- **A**sk: We have so many needs, and Jesus invites us to ask Him for anything, ranging from our *daily bread* to *His kingdom come.* We can ask for ourselves (petition) or for others (intercession).
- **Y**ield: We surrender. We ask for forgiveness and walk together with God into the rest of our day, whatever it may bring, trusting God is with us.

Enjoy

Jesus would frequently retreat from the activities and pressures of the day in order to spend time with God (Luke 5:16). Becoming a Christian can mean exploring new rhythms of connecting and communicating with God in ways that are authentic to you. Try some of these ideas.

• **Disconnect** from digital devices and find somewhere peaceful to pause. Breathe deeply, relax your body, release your stress, and center yourself in the moment with God.

• **Do** something enjoyable that makes you feel alive, like spending time outdoors, playing or listening to music, journaling, creating art, building something, singing, dancing, writing, or exercising. These moments can offer great times to praise and worship God, as you express gratitude for all the good things in God's world.

• **Develop** a rhythm of activities that feed your soul. Some may struggle to find time to connect with God spontaneously, so giving these moments priority in your week's schedule is wise. A great example is taking one day off each week to rest. The Bible calls this a *sabbath day*, and it has been a life-giving habit given by God for millennia.

Recommended Reading

BibleProject (bibleproject.com)
How to Read the Bible for All Its Worth by Gordon Fee and Douglas Stuart
How to Pray: A Simple Guide for Normal People by Pete Grieg

TWO

A New Community

*Let us consider how we may spur one another on toward
love and good deeds, not giving up meeting together,
as some are in the habit of doing, but encouraging
one another—and all the more as you see
the Day approaching.*

HEBREWS 10:24–25

We were made for community. Whereas trapped in isolation our souls tend to die, being wrapped up with others allows us to thrive. And when you step into the Christian story in response to Jesus' invitation, you not only gain a heavenly Father but also sisters and brothers, mothers and fathers, and, ideally over time, spiritual daughters and sons.

The Christian story calls this new familial community *the church*.

Search the Scriptures, and you'll find various metaphors used to describe the church. A body. A bride. A building. While each of these conveys something deeply important, they still pale in comparison to how often the Bible uses the language of *family*.

When it comes to the church, it seems God wants you to feel like you're coming *home*. And this is not some spiritual fairy tale. God's global family likely has a local home near you, where real flesh-and-blood people are bound to each other, not by DNA, but by the Holy Spirit.

Sometimes these churches gather openly in homes, caves, or cathedrals. Other times they are forced to meet in secret, underground or online. Either way, just as the Holy Spirit first animated the church at Pentecost, so too does God's presence continue to enliven these diverse churches today to help them follow in Jesus' footsteps.

So why be part of a local church?

The church is called to make disciples. Those were the last standing orders of Jesus as our commander in chief (Matt. 28:18–20). And if this language seems strange, a *disciple* is simply a student committed to becoming like their teacher. This is something akin to an apprentice to a master, only the endgame is not simply to learn a trade but to adopt their entire way of life. This is why for the last two millennia, from generation to generation, the church has passed on simple doctrines taught by Jesus and practiced simple disciplines modeled by Jesus. The goal is to learn together how to inhabit the Christian story as God intended.

What are the simple doctrines and disciplines?

The simple doctrines are a distillation of the Christian story as we described in Part 1 of this book. From its inception, the church rehearsed this story in various ways, and Christians sought to commit it to memory. Over the first few centurie, these simple doctrines were codified into memorable creeds, which all branches of the church still embrace today and often recite as they gather together around the world. Since the church are the ones entrusted to carry and commend this story, when you search for a local church, look for a community that cares about what the Bible says. Only by hearing the Christian story on repeat will God's truth become anchored in your thoughts, where it can begin to reshape the script of your life story.

As for the simple disciplines, the first Christians modeled their life together on the way of Jesus. Often they would sing songs of praise to God, tell stories about Jesus, and enjoy communal meals. For those who love food, you will be pleased to learn that feasting is a Christian discipline, because we believe that there is much to celebrate. Being thankful for what they had been given, the first Christians sought to share their wealth, giving generously to help the vulnerable of their community and toward the spread of the Christian story.

They wanted everyone to hear about Jesus.

Christians would pray continually, alone or together, contending for change as they longed for God's kingdom to come and heal their world. And in every local gathering of the church, you will still find two special traditions Jesus specifically told His followers to keep doing so that they could remember and proclaim the gospel.

The first involves water. Across the ages, new Christians have always followed Jesus' command to be baptized. They did this as an act of identifying with Him, retelling the Easter story of Jesus' death, burial, and resurrection with their own bodies by going down into the water and rising up again. The second involves a table. This is where all Christians from all walks of life gather regularly to celebrate the special meal Jesus instituted before His death. There He imbued the bread and the wine with new meaning as a way of remembering His sacrifice personally and proclaiming it publicly until He comes again. Jesus designed these sacred rhythms as a means of rehearsing the Christian story and fostering a shared life together.

Of course, as with all families, every church will do things differently and will have their own traditions that shape how they pass on these simple doctrines and disciplines. This goes some of the way to explaining why there exist so many denominations in the church. For the most part, that diversity is a strength, as these traditions dig deep wells of studied reflection and contextual experience from which we can draw. And at the end of the day, all who believe in and follow Jesus are part of the same global family, even if the church, like most other families, tends to have an eccentric uncle or combative cousin.

So what does this mean for you?

If you want to step into the Christian story, we cannot underscore enough how important a local church is in helping you grow in your new relationship with God. The church is full of diverse people who, as you walk alongside them through life, will love you, challenge you, frustrate you, and at times even lean on you in return. We need each other. God has designed the church to function like a body and, through the Holy Spirit, has given each of us different spiritual gifts (some of which may at first seem strange), so that we have to work together to glorify God and fulfill His purposes. And while you are still finding your place, the church can help you take your next steps into the story by teaching you the Bible and working through your questions.

Again, though, we must warn you. Churches are full of sinners because the gospel is a magnet for anyone who needs grace. Navigating this reality can sometimes be difficult, even hurtful, because the damage of evil continues to exist. The old adage is true: the church is more a messy hospital for sinners than a spotless museum for saints. Except for Jesus, nobody is perfect. And yet beautifully, it is through doing life with a bunch of flawed people that we all become aware of our own shortcomings, and if kindness and forgiveness flow freely, there we can help each other to stumble forward in faithfulness to Jesus.

Believe us when we say that shedding your independence to embrace this community is costly. All the best things are. And no one knows this more than Jesus. He loves the church. He gave His life for the church. As broken as the church may be sometimes, Jesus is committed to making her beautiful and a beacon of hope for the world. And Jesus invites you to take your place in that transformation. The church is a community where each of us is called to come humbly as we are and to contribute who we are. Every person is valuable, and we all have an important role to play. So if you decide to take up Jesus' invitation to step into the Christian story, here are some next steps you can take to embrace a new community gathered around the gospel.

STEPPING IN:
EMBRACING A NEW COMMUNITY

Find

Jesus tended to notice those who were on the outside of any group, and His parables often expressed His unique concern and longing for outsiders to experience God's family (Luke 15). Finding a church can look very different depending on where you live. There is likely a vast array of churches in your area, with all manner of traditions and differences. Here are a few tips for finding a healthy local church:

- **Search** online and read reviews with a generous eye.
- **Explore** a church where you already know people.
- **Ask** a Christian friend to recommend a church.
- **Look** for a church that celebrates the Bible, rehearses the Christian story, and follows Jesus' example by serving the broader community.
- **Stay** where you feel welcomed as part of the family.

Connect

The pattern of Jesus was to build deep and meaningful relationships, transforming mere acquaintances who sometimes do things together into true friends who share life (John 15:15). Even though the church is a family, meaningful relationships still take time to form. Here are ways you can go deeper with a new community:

- **Start** by regularly engaging with weekly gatherings (Sunday or otherwise).
- **See** if there are opportunities to connect socially through a smaller group.
- **Sign up** for a course at the church where you can learn more.

Serve

Jesus surprised His followers by demonstrating the shape of God's kingdom through humbly serving those around Him (Matt. 20:28). Just as each member helps in a family, Jesus wants us to contribute to a healthy church family by serving where there are needs. These are some ways you can start growing through serving at a new church:

- **Look** for ways to practically love and encourage other people.
- **Explore** existing opportunities in the ministries of the church.
- **Ask** leaders in the church how you can help.
- **Discern** what you have to contribute. Explore your talents and passions. Ask other Christians to help you identify what gifts the Holy Spirit may have given you. God intended you to serve a role in the church.

Recommended Reading

Why Bother with Church? by Sam Allberry
Life Together by Dietrich Bonhoeffer

THREE

A New Identity

If anyone is in Christ, the new creation has come:
The old has gone, the new is here!

2 CORINTHIANS 5:17

We inhabit an age when who we are is often mapped out by a series of external labels. People make superficial judgments about us and determine our value in their eyes on the basis of the color of our skin, the clothes we wear, our gender, age, or sexuality. They might even judge where we live, what we do for work, our level of education, or our politics. To survive in a world where our worth is constantly being reassessed, we often resort to a form of brand management, filtering our inner world and curating our public image so others see only what we want them to believe.

So what changes when you become a Christian?

Stepping into the Christian story involves no longer accepting labels that God has not given us. We reckon with the new reality that who we are, our true identity, and what we are worth, our true value, no longer rest on the changing tides of public opinion or personal feeling but on a more sure foundation.

We are who God says we are.

According to the Christian story, our true identity—our authentic selves—is who we were created to be *before* becoming *damaged by evil* and who we have been freed to become when through Jesus we were *redeemed by love*. And we are worth what God says we are worth. Our value was benchmarked when we were created in God's image and was extravagantly demonstrated when Jesus paid the ultimate price with His blood, a crimson currency, to secure our place in God's family.

On the question of identity, when you become a Christian, you become a whole new creation. By virtue of what Jesus has done, God no longer sees us as sinners but as saints. You launch into a new chapter of your story with the assurance that you are loved, just as you are, without having to project any semblance of being worthy. And because God secures your new identity, such that you have nothing to prove and nothing to lose, this opens up the freedom to be truly seen by others, warts and all. Jesus followers have no reason to hide who we are. We have no reason to pretend to be better than we are. Even when harsh words of critique come our way, the weight of God's affirmation tips the scales.

This, we contend, is the strongest possible anchor for human identity.

Some people may be worried this shared identity means your individuality is squashed. If everyone is meant to be more like Jesus and our old labels drop a few rungs in importance, then are we not all just going to end up looking the same?

Nothing could be further from the truth.

Every single person is uniquely created by God with all kinds of good desires, cultural inheritances, creative capacities, and singular opportunities. You are God's masterpiece, and the refinement that comes by following Jesus does not lead away from uniqueness but toward it. For as everything that distorts God's good design in you falls away with time, your unique created glory will become beautifully free for expression.

The process of working out your new identity in Jesus will no doubt take time. All of us are walking this road together. The constant challenge in a world full of superficial labels and falsehoods will be to remember who you really are. You will need all kinds of help and wisdom from trustworthy Christians who are further into the story than you are. So if you choose to take up Jesus' invitation to step into the Christian story, here are some next steps you can take to receive from God *a new identity*.

STEPPING IN:
RECEIVING A NEW IDENTITY

Know

When Jesus spoke about becoming a new creation, He compared it to being born again (John 3:3). This implies that we have to grow up into our new identity. The first step in receiving this new identity from God is all about learning how God sees you and learning to embrace it for yourself.

- **Read** the Bible and look for identity statements as God tells you who you are (for example, you are "fearfully and wonderfully made").
- **Write** a list of who God says you are, and keep it somewhere visible to serve as a constant reminder.
- **Memorize** some of these statements so habit will reshape how you see yourself.

Capture

Jesus often spoke of the destructive influence of the lies we are tempted to believe (John 8:44; 10:10). In the war for our allegiance, where our minds are the ultimate battlefield, we must daily choose to side either with God's truth about us or the enemy's lies (2 Cor. 10:4–5). These strategic pointers will help you not become a casualty.

- **Recognize** it when you hear or make identity statements about yourself (such as, *No one loves me* or *I am not good enough*).
- **Test** these statements against what God has said about your identity in Christ from the list you have already formed.
- **Isolate** the lies you are often tempted to believe so that you become aware of your points of vulnerability.

Displace

When Jesus was tempted by the snake, He responded to false ideas by challenging them with God's truth (Matt.

4:1–11). The key principle the Bible encourages when it comes to your identity is that of displacement (Rom. 12:2). When you start to believe something about yourself that disagrees with what God has said, rather than simply try to suppress the lie, instead displace it with the truth.

- **Identify** the true counter to any lie you are often tempted to believe.
- **Declare** this truth whenever that lie comes into your mind.
- **Enlist** others to remind you what God has said about you.

Recommended Reading

Victory Over the Darkness by Neil T. Anderson
The Screwtape Letters by C. S. Lewis

FOUR

A New Way to Live

Jesus replied: "'Love the Lord your God with all your heart and with all your soul and with all your mind.' This is the first and greatest commandment. And the second is like it: 'Love your neighbor as yourself.' All the Law and the Prophets hang on these two commandments."

MATTHEW 22:37–40

W hen it comes to determining right and wrong, or navigating the moral waters of life, there is no shortage of opinions. And no wonder, for the Christian story describes how we humans are prone to seizing that defining power for ourselves. When we act as the authors of our own script, morality becomes a relative endeavor, such that everyone does what is right in their own eyes. You might say that the moral maxim of our modern world is the belief that what makes you happy is the right course to chart, so long as you don't hurt anyone else along the way.

As good as this approach may seem at first, according to Jesus it is merely a shadow of how we were designed to live. It echoes what historians and philosophers have often called the *Silver*

Rule, which emerged from sages and scholars who predate Jesus.[4] They taught, "Do not inflict on others what you yourself would not wish done to you" (the harm principle).[5] Jesus' unique innovation was to call us to a higher moral vision of self-sacrifice with what has been called the Golden Rule. Jesus taught: "Do to others as you would have them do to you" (the help principle).[6] The great chasm between these two measures of right action, practically speaking, can be seen in the difference between whether your neighbor feels physically safe around you or whether your neighbor feels actively served by you.

The Christian story describes how we were *created for good*: to love God, love others, and cultivate the planet. The only problem is, having been *damaged by evil*, our heart's desires and even our consciences are no longer a reliable guide. Rather than looking outward in love to help others, we curve inward in selfishness, which means that the popular endorsement to *follow your heart* can sometimes be treacherous advice. Our moral mess is perhaps best seen in the internal fight we all experience, for even when we know what we should do, so often we fail to live up to that mark, choosing instead to say yes to something we know is wrong.

So what changes when you decide to believe in and follow Jesus?

Jesus taught that our actions are an overflow of our hearts (Luke 6:45). If we want to see our lives truly change, we need transformation from the inside out. Almost like a tree, the fruit we produce externally depends on our wellbeing internally. The Christian story describes the experience of being *redeemed by love* as a new birth that begins to transform our desires as we curve back outward toward God and others. This transformation comes through partnership as we are empowered by the Holy Spirit and supported by the church to foster a deepening relationship with God, one that nourishes us with the strength to say yes to the way of love mapped out by Jesus.

The problem is that even when we step into the Christian story, we often carry over the old habits of our moral thinking and feeling. These need to be realigned to God's good design. That process of discipling our desires and renewing our minds is rarely easy or comfortable. Jesus describes being His disciple as carrying our very own cross because sometimes following Him will feel like something in us is being killed. Why? Because it is. Sin. Selfishness. Stubbornness. In God's script, this idea of dying to self is the pathway Jesus promises will lead to a new kind of life—one where we not only love God and others but also appreciate the kind of people we become.

When it comes to relearning God's moral design, Jesus gives us a clear roadmap for a new way to be human. He is our ultimate role model and the true north for our moral compass. A good place to begin exploring what this can look like is by reading the Gospels. There love takes on flesh, giving it a particular shape, which Jesus spelled out in the roughly fifty commandments that He entreated His followers to obey. And in doing this, Jesus reminds us that true freedom is not the absence of constraints but the embrace of the right ones, like a fish to water and a train to its tracks.

So if you take up Jesus' invitation to step into the Christian story, here are some tips for following Jesus by developing new habits of walking in the way of love.

STEPPING IN:
ESTABLISHING A NEW WAY TO LIVE

Renew

Jesus said that our inner roots determine our outer fruits (Matt. 7:17–20). Therefore, any first steps in following Jesus' way of love must begin by fostering a healthy heart and conscience in relation to God. Given that humans are complex, with habits that shape our hearts, Jesus invites us to renew how we love by embracing new habits. Here are some of the regular practices Jesus built into His own life that can serve as an example to us.

- **Solitude:** After spending time with others and serving their needs, Jesus would often retreat to be alone with God and consider His own needs (Luke 5:16; Matt. 26:36–45). Take time out to reflect on how you are feeling, thinking, and acting, and ask God for the wisdom you need to help navigate what lies ahead.
- **Simplicity:** Jesus modeled a simple lifestyle, and although this is not the same as poverty, it does illustrate that most of the important things in life are not *things* (Mark 10:17–27). Take time to evaluate what you really need and consider how you can share your blessings with others rather than hoarding them for yourself.
- **Fasting:** At certain times, Jesus refrained from eating food in order to be nourished directly by God

(Matt. 4:2). You can practice fasting for special occasions or regularly, for longer periods or shorter
ones, and by cutting out all foods or just some. This
habit is a great way to break unhealthy patterns and
draw closer to God as you become aware of your
dependence upon Him for your very breath and are
stirred by hungers to pray.

- **Feasting:** At other times, Jesus celebrated life by
feasting with friends and welcoming in others who
were often left out (Matt. 26:17–19; John 2:1–12;
Luke 19:7; Mark 2:15–16). Create opportunities to
gather around tables and food in order to cultivate
relationships and express gratitude for all God has
done and the abundance that He gives.
- **Sacrifice:** Jesus demonstrated that following His
way of love requires serious sacrifices. Often saying
yes to one thing may require us to say *no* to other
things, even good things we desire (Luke 9:57–62).
Consider what things may be restricting your
ability to follow Jesus and what it could look like to
give these up. Examples might include unhealthy
dependence on substances, unbalanced work that
squeezes out life, or spending habits on things you
don't really need.

Realign

As the embodiment of God's love, Jesus demonstrated that
love is not just a feeling but an action. His life and teaching
reframes love and calls us to realign our way of life in

accordance with the fifty or so commands He entreated us to obey. These tips can help you reframe your moral thinking to realign your life with Jesus' example of love.

- **Discover:** When you read through the Gospels, you will find that Jesus has a clear roadmap for how to live. You can discover what this is by making a note of every time Jesus issues a command ("Love each other as I have loved you" or "Be merciful, just as your Father is merciful").
- **Compare:** Jesus benchmarked the standard for the way of love. Perhaps at the end of the day, reflect back, consider how your life compares to Jesus' example, give thanks for where you have done well by God's grace, and identify areas for growth.
- **Adapt:** Change is hard, but Jesus promised that the Holy Spirit will help us as we believe in and follow Him (John 14:16). As you discover new ways you want to live in God's love, keep on asking the Holy Spirit for help, and partner with Him as you embrace a new way to live (2 Peter 1:3–8).

Recommended Reading

Renovation of the Heart by Dallas Willard
You Are What You Love by James K. A. Smith
Celebration of Discipline by Richard J. Foster

FIVE

A New Purpose

*For we are God's handiwork, created in Christ Jesus
to do good works, which God prepared in advance
for us to do.*

EPHESIANS 2:10

S tepping into the Christian story in response to Jesus' invitation awakens you to a new purpose for your life. There is a sense, though, where this purpose is not entirely foreign. You could say it is, in part, something of a rediscovery of what we have neglected or forgotten, tracing all the way back to when humanity was *created for good* in God's image.

Here we touch on a concept that is thoroughly Judeo-Christian in its universality: you have a *calling*. Whoever you are, wherever you live, and whatever you choose to do for work, God has uniquely designed you for a *vocation*. A way of contributing to the human project to bring order out of chaos: building cultures, framing beauty, and fostering the fruitfulness of the earth. This is what theologians refer to as the cultural mandate, where God's first commandment in the Bible is still in effect (Gen. 1:28). Because of how God has made you, and where God has placed you, there is a specific role you are to play for good in the world (Eph. 2:10).

The Bible makes no distinction between sacred and secular work. There is as much dignity in raising kids or ploughing fields as there is in building companies or pastoring churches. The salient factor is not so much *what* we are doing (assuming it is not inherently immoral) but *for whom* are we doing it and *how* are we doing it. Are we working at our own endeavors as though working with and for God? And if so, are we going about them in a way that honors God and serves the good of all people?

Of course, there is a difference between now and when we were still in Eden. When the world became *damaged by evil*, a new purpose emerged. For those who have been *redeemed by love* through the gospel, the invitation to believe in and follow Jesus is not only to commit again to the ongoing care of creation but to join Jesus in the work of new creation. We are *sent together to heal*, spreading God's love and inviting others to step into the Christian story.

The great commission of Jesus is to make disciples wherever we go (Matt. 28:18–20). God wants to use all that you are—your gifts and talents, resources and time, opportunities and endeavors—to witness to the goodness, beauty, and truth of the gospel. We are meant to live *questionable* lives, in which our love for our neighbors sparks curiosity as to the reasons for our hope (1 Peter 3:15). Wrapped up in our answers, as we give voice to what we believe and why, our privilege is to extend Jesus' invitation, sharing the truth of the Christian story with the distinctively Christian tone of gentleness and respect.

So how can you make a start?

People often want to know God's will for their lives. What does God want me to do? You may want to know who you should marry, which course you should study, or what job you should take. Without bursting any balloons of expectation, answers to these questions rarely come thundering from heaven. Most of the time, there is no supernatural dream or vision to direct your every step. But any absence of specific guidance should not paralyze you, because God never leaves you completely in the dark. The Bible is described as a lamp for our path and a light for our feet (Ps. 119:105). Although a candle lamp may not be the high beams you wanted to light up the distant future, it does illumine enough to guide your next few steps.

Too many Christians are dragging their feet, waiting for some special revelation, when the Christian story is already packed with purposeful things for each of us to do. Although God may not reveal His specific will for your whole life right now, He certainly has revealed His general will for all Christians everywhere. So if you want to know what God wants you to do specifically, start by obeying Him generally. Over time you'll look back and realize God's hand was always guiding you along a magnificent path you could never have imagined on your own.

STEPPING IN:
LIVING WITH NEW PURPOSE

Worship

We were made to enjoy God's presence and glorify Him by serving His purposes. When Jesus prayed for us, He wanted us to have His joy and to glorify God just as He did (John 17). Worship is not something we only do in a sacred building, for since Christians are now temples of the Holy Spirit, our whole lives can become an act of worship. The more we discover who God is and learn what God has done for us, praise becomes our heart's natural overflow. So here are a few ways you can pursue a life of worship:

- **Surrender** every area of your life for God to direct.
- **Seek** God's will through prayer and reflecting on Jesus' commands.
- **Savor** God's presence throughout the day.
- **Sound** out God's praises, however that comes naturally.

Work

For three decades, Jesus worked as a carpenter, shaping the raw materials of God's creation to make them useful for human enterprise. We were created to work, bringing order out of chaos by meaningful labor that glorifies God. Whether we get paid for it or not, whether we are esteemed by the world for it or not, we are invited to do everything as if we worked for God (Col. 3:23).

- **Explore** how God has shaped your story so far and designed your passions and gifts as a clue to the kind of work you have been made for.
- **Thank** God for work. As frustrating and draining as work can be, give thanks to God for the ability to contribute who you are to the project of bringing order.
- **Acknowledge** God at work. Whether you are cleaning homes or campaigning for public office, remain conscious throughout the day that you work for God. Talk with God about people and situations in your workplace as they come to mind.
- **Influence** your workplace for good. Consider how you might model Jesus' way of love in the way you encourage others, serve humbly, stand for justice, or even steer your workplace to invest in helping the local community.
- **Do** good work. Given that we are made in God's image, what we produce can be an opportunity to reflect God's excellencies.
- **Invite** others at work to explore the Christian story with you.

Witness

Jesus constantly invited people to believe in and follow Him. As those who know firsthand how the gospel animates this life and gives hope beyond the grave, part of our purpose now is to invite others to believe in and follow Jesus. Our whole lives are meant to bear witness to the freedom and flourishing and life that comes through stepping into the Christian story. These are some healthy ways to become a helpful witness:

- **Be** a good friend who truly cares with no other agenda.
- **Forgive** freely when others wrong you.
- **Serve** the needs of people around you.
- **Pray** for opportunities to share about Jesus.
- **Think** about why the Christian story has been good news to you.
- **Practice** what you might say if someone asked you what you believe and why.
- **Learn** how to respond to common objections (see Part 3 of this book).
- **Speak** with a Christian tone of grace, gentleness, and respect.
- **Live** a life of love.

Recommended Reading

The Call by Os Guinness
Every Good Endeavor by Timothy Keller
The Master Plan of Evangelism by Robert Coleman
Evangelism in a Skeptical World by Sam Chan

TAKING THE NEXT STEPS

Now that you have a better sense of what it means to become a Christian, having counted the cost of stepping into the story for yourself, there comes a point of decision. What will you do with Jesus' invitation to believe in and follow Him?

Perhaps you still have doubts and need time to patiently address some key barriers that keep you from being able to take that step. We totally understand, which is why you are welcome now to jump into the next part of the book, "Questioning the Story."

Perhaps, though, you have heard enough to believe in and follow Jesus and want to take your first steps into the Christian story. You have come to believe that Jesus is who He claimed to be and that He is worth the cost, such that you want to embrace the new realities we have just laid out. If that is where you are on the journey toward faith, we invite you now to pray along with these words on the following page, which reflect back on the truths of the Christian story, open up a line of communication with God, and can serve as your first step into a new or deeper relationship with Him.

STEPPING IN:
A PRAYER OF RESPONSE

Dear God,

Thank You that You made me and have always loved me,
despite my failures.

Thank You for sending Jesus to die on the cross
and to overcome death.

I'm sorry for everything evil I have ever thought,
said, and done.

I'm sorry for the good things I have left undone.

Please forgive my sins, make me new, and fill me
with the Holy Spirit.

As I now choose to believe in and follow Jesus,
help me to be who You made me to be.

In Jesus' name,
Amen.

PART THREE

QUESTIONING THE STORY

The Doorway
of Doubt

A faith without some doubts is like a human body without any antibodies in it. People who blithely go through life too busy or indifferent to ask hard questions about why they believe as they do will find themselves defenseless against either the experience of tragedy or the probing questions of a smart skeptic. A person's faith can collapse almost overnight if she failed over the years to listen patiently to her own doubts, which should only be discarded after long reflection.

TIMOTHY KELLER
THE REASON FOR GOD

A long the journey toward faith, no one is exempt from getting tripped up by doubts. Whether we get caught on intellectual objections to the Christian story or find the existence of a loving God hard to square with our own personal stories of suffering, we all have hard questions for God.

Lamentably, many have been told their questions about God and the Christian story are off limits. This has spelled tragedy, for beyond the severe personal cost of suppressing doubts, it has also spawned a common misconception. Namely, that Christianity is a blind faith and to become a Christian entails surrendering reason and embracing a belief system devoid of any intellectual foundation. Nothing could be further from the truth.

God is not allergic to doubt. Jesus even seemed relatively comfortable numbering doubters amongst his dearest friends. Matthew's Gospel records how even after seeing Jesus resurrected from the dead, some of His closest followers doubted while others worshiped (Matt. 28:17), which is a strange admission if the intent of this Gospel was religious propaganda. On one occasion, Thomas, one of Jesus' apostles, was peculiarly absent when Jesus first appeared to convince the others of His resurrection. Did Thomas believe their story upon his return? No. John's Gospel records that for a whole week, Jesus left him to process his doubts (John 20:19–29). So it seems that far from suppressing doubts and demanding blind devotion, Jesus welcomed doubters and gave them the space and evidence necessary to come to their own convictions.

One of the remarkable features of the Christian story is that the same book that offers answers to life's deepest questions also opens itself up for questioning. You may be surprised to find that many of the questions we have as contemporary readers were actually posed by ancient people recorded in the Bible. As the Bible presents these stories, no attempt is made to censor the raw challenge and deep emotional register from which these questions arise. Doubt seems to be a mega theme on the journey toward faith, and the questions the Bible raises not only give voice to and validate your own, but they invite you to dive deeper into questioning the story.

God is not afraid of your questions. Why? Because if something is true, then any doubts, rather than subverting faith, should serve as a doorway to a deeper faith. For the healthy response to any doubt is to launch an open investigation. Doubts should spark you to study the reasons for faith, and upon embarking on that journey, if your curious questions are met with credible answers, then you can emerge with a more fully-orbed trust that there is a substantial *why* behind the *what* of your beliefs. Serious space should always be made for questions and questioners to explore whether the Christian story can stand up to scrutiny. Such is the hallmark of any true story.

Truth invites questioning.

So what follows is your chance to ask away at the Christian story. We have singled out seven of the most common objections and doubts that find voice all around the world. Our responses, albeit brief by design, are drafted to give you the rational scaffolding to make sense of why, despite not having all the answers, we genuinely believe the Christian story is not only something you can bank on as true news but also something you should want to bank on as good news.

Just one final note before we jump into questioning the story: as much as some of us are beholden to the notion that we are supremely rational creatures, the truth is that no human being is a logical calculator dispassionately weighing the evidence. We all possess what social psychologists call *motivated reasoning*, meaning that while facts may not care about our feelings, our feelings (or desires) tend to shape our care for the facts.[7] Whether or not we give something a fair hearing often depends on what we want to be true. So if we want to undeceive ourselves and push beyond our own biased scales to get to the truth, then we may need to apply the same level of scrutiny to our doubts as we do to the arguments for belief.

Sometimes doubts too need to be doubted.

We genuinely hope you find this section refreshing as you try to map out the intellectual and emotional space these questions inhabit and that our responses help you navigate through the doorway of doubt into a new or deeper faith in God. To help with further questions, given this is just an introductory glance into mammoth topics, there is a small offering of recommended resources after every response for you to dive deeper.

ONE

What If the Snake Was Right?

There is but one good; that is God. Everything else is good when it looks to Him and bad when it turns from Him.

C. S. LEWIS
THE GREAT DIVORCE

The tendency to doubt whether God can be trusted is a good place to start weighing our doubts. Why? Because were you to trace the genealogy of God questions back through the Christian story, you would find that no other doubt boasts such a rich pedigree. Questioning whether God is really good was ground zero of doubt in the Bible. Way back in the garden of Eden, it was the snake who first planted this skeptical seed, questioning whether we could take God at His word. When you dig beneath the surface of many of the serious objections to Christianity from Eden until now, you'll find this lingering question has fed many of those objections, almost like a root system of suspicion.

But consider the surprising flip side to this equation. Suppose there are good reasons to believe that God is supremely good. If that could be reasonably demonstrated, then the calculus changes dramatically. For then, even without comprehensive answers to every derivative objection, at the very least you can fall back to a baseline of God's goodness from which to reason.

The difficulty in navigating any territory of trust is that the terrain is shaped by our past. As young children, we tend to trust our parents without reservation, but as we grow up in a world where disappointment and betrayal taint our experience of relationships, we often find that trust is a harder-won currency. No doubt you have disappointments in life, perhaps even horrendous scars, that make it hard to believe that God is good, and we would be fooling ourselves to pretend otherwise. Even so, with eyes wide open to the disappointments and pain of life ourselves, we still believe God's goodness is the baseline of reality. Here are some of the reasons why.

To begin, there seems to be a nearly unbreakable bond between our deep intuition that goodness exists and the existence of a good God. Now this may be a little philosophical and does next to nothing to help make sense of our unmet expectations when we think about how a good God should act. Nonetheless, bear with us for a moment because there is a long-standing, strong argument for the existence of God—the moral argument—that steps soundly from our apprehension of objective moral goodness (and evil) to the existence of a cosmic moral lawgiver.[8] To spell it out negatively, without a good God it is difficult to find an anchor for objective moral values or to have a secure footing from which to oppose evil.

If we want to believe that good and evil exist beyond the changing tides of human opinion or that they are more than the blind result of our socio-evolutionary history in an ultimately purpose-less universe, then there has to be something outside ourselves to serve as the reference point for morality. Every time we denounce something as evil, like the practice of enslaving people based on the color of their skin, we believe we are making a statement of fact that is true regardless of the popular cultural beliefs of the time. The problem is that without God to serve as the arbiter between good and evil, alternative explanations are sparse. God makes good sense of our belief in objective goodness, with evil being a departure from God's good nature and design. And that we were *created for good* in God's image explains why, even if we don't believe in Him, we still apprehend the moral fabric of God's world every time we revolt against the injustices that plague our world.

A second reason to believe God is good is that there are meaningful ways to reconcile a good God with the seemingly bad things used to call His goodness into question. Were you to draw up a list of your own reasons for doubting God's character, and then investigate the responses from thinking Christians, you would discover that there are plausible ways to make sense of why a good God would allow suffering, or remain hidden, or bring about judgment. Where the struggle often lies is in taking the time to carefully consider these responses, especially when our own pain is wrapped up in the questions.

As with our own systems of justice, where innocence is assumed until proven otherwise, it only seems fair that when God is in the dock (on trial), we carefully weigh both sides of the case before making any decisions. And we need to consider that if the Christian story is true, then evil has tampered with the starting evidence of our experience, as God's good world has been corrupted.

This should at least give us pause before reasoning upward from the ground of our experiences to bring charges against God, for if the ground itself is cursed, then those experiences are not a sure and reliable eyewitness to God's character. And if the evidence against God turns out to be weaker than first believed, or if the Christian story offers a unique perspective that exonerates God's goodness, then the final verdict should overturn any original suspicion, ending with our trust in God being restored.

Beyond philosophical arguments and defensive answers, though, the best positive case for God's goodness is undoubtedly Jesus. Whereas the various events that make up the scenes of the Christian story give ample evidence that God can be trusted in His intentions toward us, none are so clear and concentrated as when God became human in Jesus. There we glimpse exactly what God is like, and the sublime moral caliber of Jesus is something impossible to capture in words, for His life was poetry in motion. Never before or since has anyone in history been so universally admired, exerting so deep a redemptive influence on hearts and minds as to transform the souls of entire civilizations. Jesus' energies were singularly directed at loving God and neighbor with all of His being. He confronted evil, sought justice, embodied compassion, extended mercy, and humbly served humanity from the cradle to the grave (and beyond). If ever there was a person who earned our trust and admiration, it was Jesus. And if Jesus is God, then when we stare at Jesus, we are staring at God. When we are drawn toward Jesus, we are drawn toward God. God's ultimate answer to questions about His character is not a bunch of words, but a person.

Jesus is heaven's response.

Reading through the Gospels dispels any lingering possibility that the snake was right to impugn God's character. Though many questions remain unanswered, where in the void of knowing we tend to drift toward doubt, Jesus anchors our belief that God really is good. In the ultimate quest for who to trust, whenever it comes down to a choice between Jesus and the snake, we are comfortable to leave you to decide for yourself.

TWO

How Could a Good God Allow Suffering?

I could never myself believe in God,
if it were not for the cross.

JOHN STOTT
THE CROSS OF CHRIST

But to our wounds only God's wounds can speak
And not a god has wounds, but Thou alone.

EDWARD SHILLITO
JESUS OF THE SCARS

None of us can escape the grim reality of evil and suffering.*
When I was just nine years old, my family suffered a terrible car accident that left Mum with serious head injuries. She would

---

* Given the scope and personal nature of this question, we opted for Dan to give an extended response, speaking first-person from his own journey. If this question is especially personal for you, we hope you find some comfort in these words.

never be the same. Alongside prematurely ending my child-hood, this tragedy was the undoing of my childlike belief in God, though I was unconscious of this at the time. Without knowing it or even being able to clearly give voice to my protest, by that roadside I had stumbled onto the most ancient and enduring objection to God.

THE PROBLEM OF EVIL

The first thinker who put pen to papyrus to clearly spell out the problem of evil was the Greek philosopher Epicurus (341–270 BC).[9] Though it may not be an accurate attribution, as the argument is put onto Epicurus's lips six centuries later by Lactantius, modern memes are replete with the version popularized by David Hume.[10] The basic argument goes like this:

> Is God willing to prevent evil, but not able? Then He is not all-powerful.
> Is He able, but not willing? Then He is malevolent.
> Is He both able and willing? Then why is there evil?

At first glance, the logic seems watertight. We have this deep-seated belief that something has gone awry, that this is not the way the world should be. Evil exists. Suffering seems wrong. And Christianity, centered around a loving God, just cannot be easily squared with family members dying of suicide, cancer, and car accidents, or with a world plagued by injustice, disaster, and abuse. Unable to make sense of why a good God would allow suffering, many people take the route I did as a boy by giving up on belief in God.

ATHEISM AND A NEW PROBLEM OF EVIL

What I came to realize during my late teenage years was that running away from God did not solve anything. Sure, given that the problem of evil is framed as a charge of inconsistency within the logic of the Christian story, getting rid of God makes that problem disappear. But evil and suffering still remain, meaning that in a world without God, I bump into an entirely new problem. Namely, how do I account for the evilness of evil, as well as our intuition that suffering is not how things ought to be? How could I explain the very thing that made me reject Christianity in the first place?

Consider the Cambodian killing fields, the gas chambers of the Third Reich, or the hulls of slaver ships that trafficked Africans across the Atlantic. Transport yourself into these situations, whether through films, stories, or memorials, and you come face-to-face with evil. But if God does not exist, then we have emptied that word of any force. With atheism, morality tends to be viewed as merely a socio-evolutionary construct, varying across time, place, and culture. One civilization says love your neighbor, another says eat your neighbor; and on atheism, morality seems relative. What this entails is that when we do stand in the presence of evil, we have lost the moral resources to call it by its name.

Moreover, if our present state of affairs is how things have always been, where in the secular story human suffering is just a brute fact of our evolutionary history, then why on earth did we develop this intuition that something has gone wrong?

Far from disproving God, then, it seems to me that our apprehension of evil as a moral reality and our intuition that the train of this world is off its tracks serve as a kind of soft evidence for the truth of Christianity. Entire books of the Bible are devoted to delving into the dark side of our human experience. What I discovered when I searched the Christian story was that Christianity makes a lot of sense in not only speaking to our pain, but in describing why we react to it the way we do.

Now the responses that do emerge from the Christian story are far from exhaustive, and anyone who claims to have a silver-bullet explanation to all of the why questions is either ignorant of their complexity or is God Himself. Nonetheless, what I hope to do now is retrace my own steps of discovery through the Christian story, where three different portraits (Genesis, Job, and Jesus) not only go a long way toward answering Epicurus's argument, but extend beyond the intellectual questions to offer serious help and hope to anyone caught in the problem of pain.

GENESIS: THE COST OF LOVE

The Christian story begins not with a world gone wrong but with a world made right. Genesis anchors our innate protest by affirming that our world was *created for good* but has tragically become *damaged by evil.* So how then does Genesis explain the origins of evil? Why does God allow suffering?

In a word, *love.* God could have created a sterile world populated by beings who only ever did what God wanted them to do, but no one can have a deep and meaningful relationship with a robot. Because God wanted to create a meaningful world, one animated by Trinitarian love, a number of indispensable features had to be built in.

First, there needed to be a stage of physical order so we could learn to harness nature for meaningful work. Being made in God's image to continue the project of bringing order from chaos, God built a world where what people do matters. As gardeners and governors of God's good world, we were created to be a part of the cause-and-effect structure, bound to our environment as embodied creatures dependent upon it for our life.

Second, humanity had to be imbued with the right degree of freedom, not only so we can be morally responsible for our actions, and so live praiseworthy lives, but also to open up the door to the possibility of love.

Imagine if, in lieu of seeking to win over the affections of my wife, instead I merely forced my love on her and coerced her into making marriage vows under the threat of death. It is safe to say that no one no one attending that wedding ceremony would be filled with warm and fuzzy feelings. Why? Because we intuitively recognize that for sacred words to mean anything they must be freely uttered. For love to mean anything, it must be freely given.

This explains why a loving God might choose to make *this* world—not a world of robots who blindly follow orders nor a world of oppressive coercion where people reluctantly obey. God chose to create a world animated by love, where humans were free to love God and love their neighbors, or to do otherwise, which is the very definition of evil.

Genesis describes what happened when God granted humanity that choice. What theologians now call *the fall* was that tragic moment in space-time history when humanity fell from love and crashed against the moral fabric of reality, whereby we, and the entire world over which we were set to govern, became *damaged by evil.*

As in any world of meaning, where what we do matters, our choices bear consequences. Akin to what happens when you try to break the law of gravity and only end up being broken by it, when humanity went against the moral grain of God's universe, there were splinters. No longer did we relate to our environment as God intended. Where once we were shielded from suffering in God's garden, now exiled from Eden, we became susceptible to disorder, disease, decay, and death.

God's good design for us was now distorted.

Sin always leads to suffering.

This does not mean, though, that the Bible endorses karma. Far from it. Though it is true that sin leads to suffering, it is equally true that not all suffering stems from sin. With the whole system now corrupted by evil, things are more complex than people simply getting what they deserve. Our sense of injustice should be provoked when seemingly indiscriminate suffering comes for the most undeserving of people. And even if it served no other purpose, their unfair suffering shouts aloud that something has gone wrong between Creator and creation.

One place where Epicurus's argument seems to go wrong is in his hidden assumption that an all-powerful God should be able to create a meaningful world where free creatures only ever freely do what God wants. The fatal flaw is the presumption that such a thing is even *possible.* For when it comes to theologians and philosophers, no one seriously believes that God's omnipotence has no logical boundaries.

There are certain things God cannot do. Why? Because they

either defy the logic of God's own mind, like the inherent contradiction represented by the creation of a square circle, or they defy God's character, which is why we are told that God cannot sin (James 1:13).[11] When it comes to the suggestion that God should be able to create billions of free creatures, none of whom ever rebel against God's good design, it seems to me that this may well fit into the same nonsensical category as the creation of a married bachelor.

Now this raises the obvious follow-up question about heaven, or God's future world in the new heavens and the new earth. If this is meant to be an everlasting place without sin, and yet freedom is indispensable in order for love to exist, then what is to stop humans from using their freedom to sin all over again? And if it is possible for a world to exist (new heavens and new earth) where free creatures do always choose God's way of love, then why not create such a world in the first place?

The answer to these questions lies in an exploration of the differences between Eden and eternity. To begin, whereas in Eden God only came periodically to be with us, as though heaven were courting earth, in eternity we are told that God will forever dwell with us, as Jesus' return finally ushers in the cosmic marriage between heaven and earth. So why was God not present all the time in Eden? Well, perhaps God's absence in Eden, and even here on earth now, serves to guard our freedom, giving us an opportunity to make a choice His constant presence wouldn't otherwise afford. For when you consider the glory of God's manifest presence, if He did not veil His glory, then the choice to worship Him would be irresistible. Whatever cosmic marriage to follow would be solely an arranged one, without the chance for us to decline. But once we have freely chosen, in response to the Holy Spirit's enabling, to reciprocate God's love, and so bind ourselves to Him for eternity, then perhaps we simply graduate, like any newly married couple, from one kind of freedom (from marriage) to another (within marriage). You could say the difference between Eden and eternity is that we transition from a freedom of breadth (options) to a freedom of depth (intimacy).

Another thing to consider is the profound difference between a finite creature being created morally innocent and that creature going on to develop moral maturity. Imagine, for instance, if a groom declared on his wedding night that he is innocent of adultery. No one at that point would be seriously impressed at his achievement, even though he is morally innocent. What would be praiseworthy is, if after fifty years of marriage, he could make the same declaration to be innocent of adultery, whether of the body, imagination, or heart. For this later kind of innocence reflects a moral maturity forged over a lifetime of fidelity, with a million daily decisions wearing a path into his character that simply couldn't have been created *ex nihilo*. Moral maturity had to develop.

One final difference between Eden and eternity lies in what we have learned having passed through the tragedy and triumph of the Christian story. While our ancestors in Eden may have been told about evil, they had no personal experience of its bitter aftertaste. That is not true of those in eternity. They will be intimately familiar with the empty promises of sin and the terrible fallout of going against God's good design. And with the coming of Jesus, they will have glimpsed glories of God's nature in ways they otherwise could never have known. Having tasted and seen the depths of God's self-giving love at the cross, drinking deeply of God's grace through the gospel, and with the snake now vanquished and his temptations silenced, it will be impossible to entertain any notion that sin is a good idea or that we need to go anywhere else to find our deepest desires satisfied. God is more than enough.

In light of these differences between Eden and eternity, it seems obvious that our world now is not the best of all possible worlds. Eternity will undoubtedly be better. But perhaps, given God's goal to create us for deep and meaningful relationships and for a role, this world now, as broken as it is, may just be the best of all possible means to finally get us to the best of all possible worlds.

When you drill down into Genesis, what you unearth is the explanation that the presence of evil and suffering, at least for a time, is the cost for love to exist. And this so-called *Free Will Defense* is but one of the various plausible answers that emerge from the Christian story.[12] The entire project of searching for answers to the problem of evil is what philosophers call *theodicy*, and although there are several other approaches, Genesis alone significantly weakens the force of Epicurus's argument. We can see *some* plausible reasons why a good God may allow evil and suffering in the general sense.

For me as a young adult, though, as illuminating as the philosophical discussion was in opening my mind, these general answers were not enough. I could get behind the idea that a world with physical and moral order was necessary for a meaningful life, and even that evil and suffering might be the cost for love to exist. But when it came to car accidents and cancer, where the victims I loved seemed innocent, I felt God needed to answer for those wrongs. That was when in the Christian story I came across the portrait of Job.

JOB: EMBRACING HUMILITY

Across the story of the Bible, a number of big names ask some hard questions of God when it comes to their suffering. Chief among them is Job, who was a relatively good guy whose life was suddenly ripped apart. In short succession, Job's ten children were crushed by a collapsing house and entombed by the rubble, his wealth was stolen away by enemy raiders or destroyed by natural disasters, and his health disappeared as his body was ravaged by skin disease. To top it all off, his wife finally turned on him, jeering at him to give up his faith in God. Naturally, as we all do in the midst of personal crisis, Job begins to wonder why and starts to question the justice of the way God allows suffering. And when God eventually steps into the story, rather than answering Job's questions, God asks sixty-four of his own, starting with these (Job 38:2–5):

> "Who is this that obscures my plans
>   with words without knowledge?
> Brace yourself like a man;
>   I will question you,
>   and you shall answer me.
>
> "Where were you when I laid the earth's foundation?
>   Tell me, if you understand.
> Who marked off its dimensions? Surely you know!"

When I first read this barrage of questions, I thought God's response was rather cruel. How was this a compassionate answer, or an answer at all, to why Job was suffering? Eventually, I got the point. What God was trying to do with this cosmic quiz was give

Job some perspective on the enormity of what it means to govern a universe from God's chair. By comparison, as finite creatures, there are innumerable things we either do not or simply cannot know.

This point came home to me a number of years ago when I had to take my firstborn son, Josiah, for the next round of needles in his immunization schedule. He was only eighteen months old, and because with toddlers you only get one stab at the task (pardon the pun), the doctor and nurse said they would inject the two needles simultaneously, one in each arm. They had me sit Josiah on my lap, and as he stared up at me lovingly, they counted down and quickly plunged in their needles. I will never forget those next few moments. Josiah's little body winced with pain, and his precious eyes filled with tears. Just like Job, he looked up at me terribly confused and feeling betrayed. I was his daddy. From all of our adventures, he knew my strength and how I could easily have defended him from the medical staff. And he knew the depths of my love from all the time I spent looking after him, playing, talking, and cuddling. Josiah just could not fathom why his powerful and loving daddy didn't intervene to keep him from suffering, let alone why I paid the doctor afterward for having inflicted this torture.

Obviously, as a reasonably-educated adult with a working knowledge of immunology and the dangers of viral or bacterial infection and disease, I had good reasons for allowing Josiah to suffer this momentary pain to secure for him a safer future. But there was simply no way I could relate those reasons to Josiah because, as a toddler, he could not comprehend them. And if that was true for an eighteen-month-old boy and his thirty-year-old dad, imagine how much more true would that be of a finite human being compared to an infinite and all-wise God.

There is an unbridgeable gap between us and God. God doesn't only know the answers to all the questions He asked Job. He doesn't only know the movement of every atom in the universe, along with the number of hairs on my head (which gets easier to count every year). What truly sets God apart is how He can look through the corridors of time to see the butterfly effect of every event. Because God knows every possible future, only God is in a position to know when and how to intervene to secure the best outcome.

So if we learn anything from Job's portrait, when it comes to addressing our specific *why* questions, God doesn't provide exhaustive answers. What God does instead is invite us to lean into His bigness and recognize that as far as the heavens are above the earth, so are God's thoughts above our own (Isa. 55:9). We are invited to trust that when it comes to our suffering, God has good reasons for allowing it, reasons of which we are simply unaware.

For me, this was a tough pill to swallow. I could get behind the idea that if God exists then He is bigger than me. But I struggled to believe God was worthy of my trust or see how the things that had happened to my family could ever serve any purpose or good. Unlike Josiah sitting on my lap, I thought I had no evidence that God really cared for me as a loving heavenly Father. But that discovery came in the third portrait, when I finally made it to the stories about Jesus.

JESUS: GOD'S RESPONSE
TO OUR EVERY HEART CRY

Jesus offers something far richer than the speculations of philosophers. For although Jesus does not bypass the mind or stifle our search for answers, He takes aim at the heart. Why? Because underneath the guise of logical arguments, there so often lurks a deeper emotional problem of evil. This emotional element makes the problem of evil especially thorny, for there is always a questioner behind the question, and we all have a story of inner turmoil.

Jesus is God's response to our every heart cry. What I discovered from reading through the Gospels is that Christianity offers far more than a mere explanation for our suffering. For through this portrait, far above any of the other religious or secular stories I have encountered, Jesus gives us not only the reasons why we can entrust our suffering into God's hands, but also the resources to find meaning, hope, and healing through our suffering.

How?

The first thing that gripped me about Jesus was the deep well of compassion and grief that poured out of Him in reaction to our pain. I guess somewhere along the line I had taken up the idea that if God does exist, then He is cold and uncaring, cloistered far away from our cries here on earth. But John's Gospel records a powerful scene where one of Jesus' dear friends, a young man named Lazarus, fell sick and died (John 11:1–44). Upon hearing the news, Jesus took His disciples to the funeral in Bethany, where being confronted with Lazarus's two grieving sisters, Mary and Martha, God's reaction to our suffering was on public display.

Jesus wept.

A grown Jewish man, dignified as a renowned rabbi, broke down and sobbed before the gathered crowd. Though in the past I had been tempted to believe my compassion ran deeper than God's response, I realized from this story that my initial assessment was misguided. As a heavenly Father to His earthly children, God *feels* deeply for us. He sees our struggles. He is grieved by our suffering. Perhaps one day, when the dust settles on the pain of this life, we will all come to realize the tears we shed for the suffering of this world were never ours alone. They were only ever on loan from those deep wells of God's compassion.

Next, beyond merely stepping into our grief, Jesus directed us to look through our tears toward a future hope. Tapping into a deep vein that spreads across the pages of the New Testament, Jesus promised that one day, the source of all of our sadness will be undone. Evil will be ended, suffering eclipsed, and death overthrown. The last pages of the Bible even paint the picture that, for all who were willing to come to Jesus, whatever tears remain from our suffering in this world will be wiped away by God's own hand (Rev. 21:4). All of this is what Jesus hinted at near Lazarus's grave when he spoke of Himself as the resurrection and the life (John 11:25).

The great gift of this future hope is how it recasts our suffering in the present. Our suffering is not the last word. And on balance, when compared to eternity, our present pain is set to be dramatically outweighed on the scales of time and magnitude, as though comparing a momentary cup of tears to the endless ocean of joy that will be found in God's presence (Rom. 8:18; 2 Cor. 4:17). By helping us to reckon with eternity, Jesus puts our pain into perspective. This is not the way things will always be. So we can take heart.

Only Jesus' promised future hope was not merely some form of escapism. With His face set against evil and suffering, Jesus' public ministry described in the Gospels was characterized by the announcement that God is coming near to make things return to their rightful order. As a foretaste and sign of that future world, Jesus performed miracles of physical healing, rebuked existing powers for their abuse of position, and sacrificially served those whom no one else regarded as worthy of attention. The Gospels portray God's response to the problem of evil as one of a war against all corruption, where Jesus treated suffering, sickness, and death as enemies to human freedom and flourishing and life. To Jesus, evil and suffering weren't just something to be ignored or endured but something to be confronted and alleviated as part of God's kingdom coming to earth. This was Jesus' legacy to His followers.

To say that evil and suffering were neither part of God's good design nor will be part of God's future world does not mean that they are beyond His reach for some present purpose. Even though God may not stand directly behind people's evil actions or the suffering we experience bound to a broken world, God can redeem these events to serve a meaningful purpose. The dominant image of the New Testament when it comes to suffering is that of a fire, which can either be used to forge or destroy (1 Peter 1:6–9; 4:12–13). Suffering has that power, depending on where we turn when the heat is on.

If we give up running from God and run toward Him instead, the Bible promises that God will weave even our darkest nights of the soul into a grand tapestry for our good (Rom. 8:28). How exactly? I don't know. The grace for asking that question long enough, though, is that you gain retrospect as a teacher. Looking back now, I can see at least some of the ways God meaningfully used the scars of my past to shape me for today. Whether it was to confront my choices, carve out my character, build reservoirs of empathy, or hone my perspective, my suffering has not often been wasted. But even here, I am only seeing in part, as through a glass dimly. A thick cloud of mystery shrouds the specifics, and some of my own questions for God go unanswered. Yet what finally melted my skepticism, the thing that enabled me to lean into God's bigness in this fog of the unknown, was the discovery in the Gospels that I was not wandering there alone.

This is where Jesus stands head and shoulders above the gods and heroes of religious and secular stories. Christianity describes a God who is not untouched by our pain. God chose to forsake the safety of heaven to enter earth's fray. And the passion of the Christ, the suffering of Jesus, when you wade through all the gory details of His torture and execution, is a profound declaration—nay, a demonstration—of the depths of God's love for us.

God's answer to our suffering, at least in part, is to step in and suffer. Jesus did that, experiencing excruciating agony, because He loved us so much He would rather endure the punishment of hell than enjoy heaven without us. Jesus is a God who has so endured evil and become familiar with suffering that, even after His resurrection, even on into eternity, He wears the scars to prove it.

Even when we don't have all the answers as to why God allows us to suffer, the Cross of Christ shouts over all our doubts that we are not abandoned and that we are profoundly loved. If God is big enough to outplay evil by defeating it through the Cross, somehow reversing the greatest tragedy in history to serve as a vehicle of salvation, then who knows what God is capable of doing when we entrust our suffering into His hands?

RUNNING TOWARD GOD

Although the impulse to run away from God is understandable, I have found that this doesn't seem to solve our true dilemma. The problem of pain remains; only, in a script without God, we lose the ground from which to protest it and the hope to overcome it. Through my own journey, I have become convinced that the Christian story offers the most substantial answer to the problem of evil and suffering, making sense of our deep intuition that something is wrong, animating our desire to challenge evil and alleviate suffering, and promising that a God with scars will be with us in our pain, even making something of us through the pain, until its final eclipse in God's future world.

Even if I didn't have many good reasons to believe Christianity was true, and I was simply wagering on what I wanted to be true, when confronted with the problem of pain, I would genuinely choose to live as though the Christian story is true. For if I am to face suffering either way, I would much rather suffer with Jesus than suffer without Him.

Recommended Reading

The Problem of Pain by C. S. Lewis
A Grief Observed by C. S. Lewis
Where Is God in All the Suffering? by Amy Orr-Ewing
Walking with God through Pain and Suffering by Timothy Keller
Why? by Sharon Dirckx

THREE

Why Isn't God More Obvious?

God has given evidence sufficiently clear for those with an open heart, but sufficiently vague so as not to compel those whose hearts are closed.

BLAISE PASCAL
PENSÉES

Why does God make it so hard to believe in Him? This isn't just a big question for atheists and agnostics who don't believe in God. Even Christians often find themselves full of doubts, fueled by times when God just doesn't seem as *real* as we think He should.

People the world over struggle to believe in a God they cannot see. Our secular age has trained us to think that the only things to be accepted as real are those that can be proved objectively by undeniable evidence. And when it comes to the God question, many feel the evidence just doesn't stack up. If God really wanted everyone to believe in Him, why didn't He make His existence more believable?

Surely being omnipotent means God would have avenues of revealing Himself that are capable of convincing everyone that He exists. God could tear open the sky in a cosmic version of peek-a-boo, or He could appear on live television to answer the questions of late-night comedians. God could write our names with constellations in the night sky or genetically stamp "Made by God" as a birthmark on the bottoms of our feet. But since God does not reveal Himself in these crystal-clear ways, we are tempted to believe God either isn't there or doesn't care.

So why isn't God more obvious?

One way to think about this question is to explore whether God is perhaps more obvious than we give Him credit for. The Christian story speaks about how God has not left Himself without testimony (Acts 14:17) but has revealed Himself through nature, human experience, and history. And from the reflection on the available evidence, Christian thinkers who work in the field of natural theology advance roughly two dozen or so arguments for the existence of God that span various academic disciplines.[13]

In the world of philosophy, for example, just over a century ago, the Austrian philosopher and atheist Friedrich Nietzsche famously announced that God is dead in philosophy.[14] Today, though, if you were to survey top-flight philosophy faculties around the world, you would discover something of a revival of belief in God. Whether from the rehashing and strengthening of ancient arguments or the development of entirely new ones, the case for God's existence over the past fifty years has been ably made and defended in literature and at academic conferences by Christian philosophers like Alvin

Plantinga, Richard Swinburne, and William Lane Craig.[15] This theistic renaissance in philosophy has been so pronounced that it sparked Quentin Smith, a renowned atheist philosopher, to reverse Nietzsche's pronouncement and confess that God is not dead in philosophy but is alive and well in this academic stronghold.[16]

The case for the existence of God can also be argued from the study of nature. The Bible claims that creation bears the fingerprints of its Creator (Ps. 19:1–2; Rom. 1:20). And beyond the personal way this claim is substantiated whenever the sheer beauty of nature floods us with awe, science too can play a role for those seeking greater objectivity. Over the past century or so, the systematic study of our cosmos, whether through a telescope or a microscope, has yielded fascinating discoveries that serve up solid reasons to believe in God. One would be the discovery that our universe had an absolute beginning, when everything came from nothing.[17] Cosmologists are also documenting how finely tuned our universe was, with initial conditions so exquisitely calibrated to allow for intelligent life.[18] Biologists have mapped the complex structure of DNA, discovering that biology is governed by something much like a language of life.[19] When you put together the pieces of these remarkable discoveries, the appearance of design in nature emerges unmistakably.

These are but two disciplines among many, and when you dive into field after field, there is a veritable smorgasbord of evidence and arguments of various strengths, some generally pointing toward the existence of God and others more specifically lending weight to the truth of the Christian story. Despite what many of us have been told, belief in God is not some blind leap into the dark. By simply following the trail of evidence to where it leads,

Christian faith seems to be a rational step into the light. And yet still, despite the reasonably strong cumulative case for God, many who have studied these arguments remain unconvinced.

So why has God left room for doubt?

While being conscious not to project motives onto anyone, perhaps one reason God may not seem obvious has to do with whether or not we want God to exist. According to Genesis, humanity started hiding from God behind fig leaves and fern bushes long before God ever seemed hidden from us. And if the Christian story is true and our hearts are *damaged by evil*, then perhaps we can wear something of a blindfold when it comes to the God question (2 Cor. 4:4). What if sometimes we can't see God simply because we don't want to (Rom. 1:18)?

Psychology has carefully substantiated the notion that we all possess motivated reasoning.[20] Our reason often only serves to justify our desires. It may be true that some Christians only believe in God for the psychological benefits, but that sword of critique cuts both ways. There are plenty of potential psychological motivations for not wanting God to exist. Perhaps we prefer to remain in the dark because we think God will cramp our moral style. Maybe something in our past provokes us to feel guilty or ashamed, and so we don't like the idea of giving an account before God. Or perhaps we have such a distorted view of God that we rightly revolt against the existence of a monster.

Now again, this is not to cast suspicion on anyone's motives. No one should be accused of psychologically burying God for their own ends unless that is something they freely confess. But if it is possible that our confirmation bias has set the bar of evidence unreasonably high, then it is at least worth considering how what you want to be true about God might be coloring your take on the evidence.

But let us shift gears here. Because the simple truth is that as much as we might sometimes hide from God, the Christian story freely admits that God hides from us, even from those who serve Him faithfully. The songbook of Israel records the lament, "Why, LORD, do you stand far off? Why do you hide yourself in times of trouble?" (Ps. 10:1). And this is not a stand-alone episode. There are scores of people throughout the Bible who experience divine silence and dark nights of the soul, when God fails to live up their expectations.

So why does God hide?

One reason may be that God desires more than mere belief. No doubt God could reveal Himself so obviously that everyone is forced to believe that He exists. But what if God's endgame, the goal of His revelation, has less to do with simply believing *that* God exists propositionally and more to do with leading us to believe *in* God personally? After all, given that the Bible records that even the demons believe God exists (James 2:19), it seems entirely possible that mere belief in God's existence might do nothing to engender the response God so desires, which is a deep and meaningful relationship.

Think about it this way. Imagine a boy was interested in a girl. What would happen if, having never talked to her, he just turned up at her house, told her he had been watching her for years, knows everything about her, and wants to spend forever with her? He would probably end up in police custody, and she would run away—fast!

So what if the same is true about God? If God turned up with overwhelming force, sure, we might believe that He exists, but our preconceptions about Him, our spiritual blindness, and even the darkness of our desires might only end up hardening our hearts toward Him. We would lose the light and life and love of being with God for eternity, all because God came on too strong. So perhaps, like in Søren Kierkegaard's parable of "The King and the Maiden," God comes more humbly, even veiling His majesty, in order to woo us.[21] Since God is way bigger and better than we realize, able to look into all possible futures to know how we would react, perhaps God carefully curates when and how and to what degree He reveals Himself personally in order to open up the greatest chance of a deep and meaningful relationship with each of us for all eternity.

So God hides because He loves us and so desires more than mere belief.

Perhaps a second reason God may choose to hide is to help us become heavenly rather than hellish beings. Now we raise this being sensitive to the reality that it may hit a nerve for those of us who are wrestling with disappointment with God. Still, what if God chooses not to live up to our expectations because His remaining hidden is the best thing for us right now? To offer a trivial example, we might want to eat pizza or ribs nearly every night for dinner, but our hungers alone are not a trustworthy guide for what will make us healthy. Like any good parent, God prioritizes what we need over what we want. Rather than giving us the experience of His presence we desire, perhaps God gives us the kind of presence we require, where any perceived absence is purposeful on God's part, designed to help us become who we are meant to be.[22]

Imagine a father tasked with teaching his boys to take big steps independently. When the boys are young, the father may delight to carry them down the road, and any onlookers would think this scenario cute. Only what if those boys were now teenagers or, worse, adults? If the father still has to carry them, then at some point, the picture becomes strange, and the father has obviously failed in his task.

And when we transpose that thought experiment into the Christian story, God's endgame is even more grand. Our task in God's future world is to govern alongside Jesus. That's a serious calling that requires some serious training. So given all that God knows, perhaps He makes His presence or absence felt in accordance with what will serve in our preparation to step into that future.

When God seems absent? He is working toward this plan.

When suffering comes? God is working it into His plan.

When your prayers seem unanswered? God is sticking to the script.

As counterintuitive as it may seem, God loves us so much that He is willing to hide His presence here and now in order to get us ready to enjoy His presence there and then. Even when we want more, perhaps even when He wants us to have more, God is committed, as a good heavenly Father, to giving us what we need in order to become heavenly rather than hellish beings. And at the core of becoming a heavenly being is learning God's rhythms of love. Perhaps this explains God's hiddenness best, as though God is playing a cosmic game of hide-and-seek. Since love involves the constant pursuit of the other, God never stops inviting us to play, in order that by being encouraged to constantly seek after Him, we might learn the way of love.

As is so often the case, though, God's answer to this big question is Jesus. At the heart of the Christian story is the claim that Jesus is the invisible God made visible. Jesus is the hidden God made obvious. And that is a claim that is open to historical investigation. You can explore the evidence for Jesus' beautiful life, His sacrificial death, and His miraculous resurrection to conclude for yourself whether God has made Himself known in history.

What Jesus reveals through the Christian story is how God is good even when He seems absent. When Jesus died on the cross for our sin, just like us when we experience dark nights of the soul, He felt God's absence. He even quoted a famous psalm from King David: "My God, my God, why have you forsaken me?" (Ps. 22:1). But even when God seemed absent, in that very moment He was present. Jesus' self-sacrificial death on our behalf was the greatest possible display of His divine love for us. He showed us exactly what we are worth to Him as His arms were stretched wide upon the beams of the cross. And all of this had a purpose. God was fulfilling the eternal plan, redeeming us in love and extending salvation to anyone who believes so that we can all experience the freedom and flourishing and life of being with God for eternity.

Jesus is the reason we can trust that God really is there and that He does care, even when right now, perhaps, He may not seem as obvious or real as we would like Him to be.

Recommended Reading

When God Isn't There by David Bowden
The Hiddenness of God by Michael C. Rea

FOUR

Has Science Disproved God?

The prohibition of science would be contrary to the Bible, which in hundreds of places teaches us how the greatness and the glory of God shine forth marvelously in all His works, and is to be read above all in the open book of the heavens.

GALILEO GALILEI,
"LETTER TO MADAME CHRISTINA OF LORRAINE,
CONCERNING THE USE OF BIBLICAL QUOTATIONS
IN MATTERS OF SCIENCE"

For many in our secular age there exists an underlying belief that there is a zero-sum game between two competing options for making sense of the universe: faith versus fact, religion versus reason, God versus science. When you survey how many high-profile scientists are vocal critics of religion, you could easily form the impression that modern science has progressively chased away the superstitious shadows of faith and that well-established theories in cosmology and biology have done away with any need for a Creator. So is it true that in cosmic chemistry God and science cannot mix?

Has science disproved God?

To explore the territory of this question, let us start by making a simple observation. If God and science are at war, then you would expect to find a certain demographic of casualties strewn across the intellectual battlefields—namely, scientists who believe in God. For if science had buried God, then any scientist worth their salt would surely give up on their religious beliefs.

The only problem? The facts suggest otherwise.

A great many high-profile scientists are also believers in God. Francis Collins directs the United States National Institute for Health. Jennifer Wiseman serves as the Senior Project Scientist for NASA's Hubble Space Telescope. Gerhard Ertl was awarded the Nobel Prize in Chemistry in 2007. And beyond these selective examples, a survey of Nobel-Prize winners in the hard sciences across the twentieth century reveals that more than 85 percent self-identified as Christian or religiously Jewish, outing themselves as believers in God.[23] So from this simple observation, we can draw a simple conclusion: if science has disproved God, then someone forgot to tell an awfully large number of prize-winning scientists.

Of course there are points of tension between religion and the scientific project. Perhaps one reason high-profile atheistic scientists are critical of religion is the unhelpful way some Christians tend to try to plug God into scientific questions. Consider how the ancients, due to an ignorance of the laws that govern our universe, invoked the gods to make sense of natural phenomena. Lightning was Zeus. Thunder was Thor. And sadly, too often you can find well-meaning Christians who adopt this god-of-the-gaps approach, invoking God to explain things in nature we don't yet understand.

Now what is sad about this anti-scientific impulse is that it runs counter to the long heritage of Christians who have been serious scientific thinkers. In fact, throughout history, Christianity played a key role in the rise of modern science.[24] Almost all of the fathers of the modern fields of science were believers in God, Jesus, and the Christian story. Isaac Newton. Johannes Kepler. Michael Faraday. And their Christian faith was not incidental to their science. They took seriously Jesus' great commandment to love God with their mind (Matt. 22:37) and the cultural mandate in Genesis to subdue, rule over, and make earth fruitful (Gen. 1:28). Johannes Kepler believed in his study of mechanics that he was thinking God's thoughts after Him.[25] Isaac Newton argued that his *Principia Mathematica* was intended to move people from perceiving the rational order of the universe to believing in God.[26] And so C. S. Lewis sums up in a single sentence what historians and philosophers of science justify in lengthy scholarly tomes: "Men became scientific because they expected Law in Nature, and they expected Law in Nature because they believed in a Legislator."[27] For these brilliant pioneers, far from being a hindrance to their scientific endeavors, it would seem that God inspired their science.

Not only did the Christian story provide the philosophical soil and motivational fertilizer out of which modern science largely grew, but many of the subsequent discoveries of science, far from pointing away from God, make more sense in light of God's existence. For instance, the discovery that our universe—space, time, matter, and energy—is not eternal but had an absolute beginning at some finite point has strengthened one of the most famous philosophical arguments for God's existence: the Kalam Cosmological Argument.[28] So too has the discovery of the highly improbable calibration of the initial conditions of our universe to allow for intelligent life led to the development of a teleological line of reasoning known as the Fine-Tuning Argument.[29] When combined with discoveries like the surprising way abstract mathematics maps onto the physical world,[30] or the way biological organisms are comprised of coded information systems,[31] our universe bears the unmistakable appearance of design. This ordered structure in our cosmos is what recently prompted Ard Louis, professor of theoretical physics at Oxford University, to observe in conversation with Morgan Freeman, "I think the more we learn about the world, it points more toward God, rather than less."[32]

So far from burying God, if anything it seems that science is resurrecting a rational belief in God. And while science can unearth a great deal about the history of our universe, when it comes down to it, disproving God is simply not in its purview. As huge a gift as the tool of science is to the tool belt of knowledge, not every question has a scientific answer. Science has limits. Being bound to purely observe and measure the physical universe, science has no access to the metaphysical. It cannot say whether God does or does not exist. Furthermore, it cannot move from describing what is to pontificating about what ought to be. Nor can it repeat the past to prove what did or did not happen. So as soon as we step into questions of metaphysics, ethics, or even human history, we simply move beyond the authority of the hard sciences to speak.

Where many who pose this scientific objection ultimately get tripped up is by confusing different types of explanations. Suppose we were to ask you why you are reading this book and you answered, "Well, the ink blots on these pages are refracting the light from the sun, which then passes through the lenses of my eye. There the arrangement of the letters are translated into electro-chemical signals, which my brain interprets via centers for language and memory, forming them into coherent thoughts that convey meaning to my conscious mind." Now we may be impressed at your wit, but you have answered a slightly different question. You have provided a scientific or mechanistic explanation—the *how*. What we were really asking for was a personal explanation, or an explanation of agency—the *why*. To which the answer might be something like, "Because I am searching for answers to life's deepest questions."

The how and the why, the mechanism and the agency, are not competing explanations. These are complementary explanations. Because as much as we can learn about the process of reading from science, we can learn nothing about why you are reading from that same enterprise. For that, *you* have to speak. And the same is true when it comes to science and God. Science can tell us a great deal about *how* the universe operates, but it cannot tell us *why* it exists.

For that, God has to speak.

And when it comes to God and the Christian story where He speaks, we know of no serious scientific reason to disbelieve anything Jesus has said about who you are, why you are here, and where you are going. If anything, science should give you some good reasons to tune in more carefully.

Recommended Reading

God's Undertaker: Has Science Buried God? by John Lennox
Can Science Explain Everything? by John Lennox
The Story of the Cosmos: How the Heavens Declare the Glory of God,
    Paul M. Gould and Daniel Ray, gen. eds.
God's Crime Scene by J. Warner Wallace

FIVE

Can I Trust the Bible?

The evidence for our New Testament writings is ever so much greater than the evidence for many writings of classical authors, the authenticity of which no one dreams of questioning. And if the New Testament were a collection of secular writings, their authenticity would generally be regarded as beyond all doubt.

F. F. BRUCE
THE NEW TESTAMENT DOCUMENTS: ARE THEY RELIABLE?

Central to being able to step into the Christian story is the confidence that what you have read about Jesus reliably represents history, such that it is neither a hoax nor some fanciful myth. For many modern readers, this ancient story can appear littered with questionable claims and events, ranging from the creation of the world and miracle stories to the existence of spiritual beings and people rising from the dead. And when you overlay the story with the common charge of being outdated and irrelevant—nothing but a relic littered with errors and inconsistencies—we can see why the Bible faces a crisis of credibility.

As a witness to the events of Jesus' life, the Bible has been in the dock for centuries. And if we are going to subject it to our own trial, it helps to get a sense of the unique shape of this book, for the Bible is far more sophisticated than many of us may realize. To offer something of a thumbnail sketch, the Bible is a compilation of sixty-six books written over 1500 years by roughly forty different authors who wrote in three languages (Hebrew, Aramaic, and Greek), inhabited three continents (Europe, Asia, and Africa), and represented the whole spectrum of the social order including fishermen, shepherds, doctors, priests, historians, warriors, philosophers, statesmen, scholars, and even kings. The diversity of these authors is matched only by the veritable smorgasbord of literary genres they incorporated: historical narratives, national chronicles, sermons, letters, songs, poetry, parables, architectural designs, travel diaries, inventories, geographical surveys, eyewitness accounts, family trees, population statistics, biographies, and legal documents. What makes the Bible a historical anomaly is how, despite such diversity, these individual books come together to form a literary constellation of meaning, or a mosaic where out of the disparate parts a unified story emerges. This is one reason among many why Christians believe the Bible is not only trustworthy as a roadmap to reality but also inspired by God, because it bears the fingerprints of a divine composer.

At the same time, the complexity of the Bible raises challenges. We may be convinced that the whole Bible is inspired, and that is trustworthy and true, but given our distance in time and culture from the world of the Bible, in some cases it can be hard to neatly interpret the intended meaning. Was the author offering a divine take on history? Or was it a clever tale to expose bad motives? Or perhaps an allegory to unveil hidden truths about who God is and who we are? This is why Christians disagree about books like Jonah, Job, and the early chapters of Genesis. Are they history? Or theological poetry? Or something in between? Sometimes we just don't know what genre some sections represent, and while we can discern the core message, the details remain an open question for humble discussion. Now for our money, Jesus spoke of Adam and Eve, Cain and Abel, Noah, Abraham, and Jonah as real people who actually lived. But this is where we get to the crux of the question about trusting the Bible, because so much of what Christians believe about the Bible is based on Jesus.

Archaeology only offers a limited window into the past since most of history has been destroyed by the sands of time. Though the events of the Old Testament have a good track record of being vindicated by archaeological findings,[33] and the science of textual criticism gives us confidence that these ancient texts have been well preserved from intentional corruption,[34] the scarcity of external sources means that less than one percent of the ancient world is open to us. As such, it seems unreasonable to expect to find external verification for everything in the Bible. The old adage still stands: the absence of evidence is not evidence of absence.

Yet the truth is not lost to us. Jesus opens an avenue for establishing the Bible's trustworthiness through a legitimate appeal to authority. For if Jesus was who He claimed to be (God become human) and if Jesus verified Scripture as being trustworthy as a book from God, then without any serious defeaters to disprove the Bible's reliability, we have good reason to take Jesus at His word and accept His view of Scripture. So rather than verify the reliability of the whole Bible, we can narrow the test sample to the Gospels to investigate whether they stand up to scrutiny as the primary historical sources on Jesus.

So can we trust the Gospels?

The first reason why you can trust that the Gospels record reliable eyewitness testimony about Jesus is that the stories are loaded with fleshy details that only eyewitnesses would know. Imagine how extraordinarily difficult it would be, without the help of Wikipedia or Google Maps, to get incidental details right about a people and a place with which you were completely unfamiliar? Yet the Gospels, which likely were not written in Jerusalem but in other cities of the Roman Empire, are packed with accurate intimate knowledge of the architecture, road systems, town names, city elevations, religious customs, political tensions, food, agriculture, botany, and even popular names of the people who lived in Galilee and Judea at the time of Jesus.[35] This feature is precisely what distinguishes the canonical Gospels (Matthew, Mark, Luke, and John) from the controversial gnostic Gospels (Thomas, Peter, Judas, Mary, Philip). These latter works were rejected from being part of the Bible's canon not only because they were written over a century after the events they supposedly record, meaning they couldn't possibly have come from the apostles, but also because, unlike the canonical Gospels, they lacked any of the relevant details you would expect if they contained reliable eyewitness testimony.[36]

A second reason you can trust the Gospels is that the content is simply too counterproductive to serve as religious propaganda. If the goal of the authors was to convince Jews, Greeks, or Romans to sign up to believe in and follow Jesus, then many unbecoming details would have been airbrushed out before the Gospels went to print. For instance, if the Gospels are meant to establish the authority of the apostles, it hurts their credibility to be painted as a bunch of bumbling fools on nearly every page. After all, Peter fails to walk on water (Matt. 14:28–33), denies Jesus three times (Luke 22:54–62), and even provokes Jesus to refer to him as Satan (Matt. 16:23), which is not exactly a resume you want announced by the emcee before you stand up for a speaking gig. If propaganda was the point and you wanted to establish Jesus as God, then centering the biographies around His execution would be a spectacular exercise in self-sabotage, since everyone in the first century would have understood a crucified God to be a complete contradiction in terms.[37] So when one considers how brutally honest the Gospels are about innumerable embarrassing features, the most plausible explanation is that these blemishes bear testimony to their authenticity. They report what really happened.

A third reason you can trust the Gospels is that the testimony recorded was high stakes. Worshiping a man as God was considered an act of extreme blasphemy for the first-century Jews who comprised Jesus' inner circle. Not only did Jesus' divine claims cause His half siblings to reject Him as mad (Mark 3:21), but it sparked the religious establishment to want Him executed (John 10:33). Blasphemy was a big deal. Eternal condemnation was on the line if they were wrong about Jesus, and there seems to be no temporal gain for lying about it either. Jesus' followers eschewed riches, often faced beatings and imprisonment, and were chased away from their homes and livelihoods for believing in and following Jesus. We have good historical sources to confirm that at least four of the apostles were martyred for preaching about Jesus and no evidence that any of them recanted their testimony.[38] That they were willing to face intense hardships and endure brutal executions makes no sense unless they genuinely believed the veracity of their testimony, especially in light of the eternal cost if they were wrong. So the high-stakes nature of their testimony, along with the admirable character of the apostles, all speak to the Gospels' authenticity.

Perhaps the most compelling reason to trust the Gospels, though, is the colossal figure of Jesus Himself. Anyone who could invent such a moral genius would have to be a literary luminary beyond the likes of Shakespeare. There is a gravity to His teaching, a singular caliber to His life, and the ring of truth in His redemptive interactions with the men and women of the Gospels. If Jesus did not exist—or was unhinged or some evil imposter and not who He claimed to be—then it is a nearly impossible task to explain the source of the revolutionary teachings and explosion of the Jesus movement.

Now none of these reasons to trust the Gospels placate all the objections to the Bible. Each barrier you have should be carefully considered with good resources and patient investigation. What our reasons do offer, though, is a starting point. Because if Jesus did rise from the dead historically as these sources testify, then we have no reason to deny the supernatural out of hand and every reason to start taking Jesus seriously, including what He said about the rest of Scripture as inspired and trustworthy.

Recommended Reading

Is Jesus History? by John Dickson

Why Trust the Bible? by Amy Orr-Ewing

Can We Trust the Gospels? by Peter J. Williams

Cold-Case Christianity by J. Warner Wallace

Jesus and the Eyewitnesses by Richard Baukham

SIX

Did Jesus Really Rise from the Dead?

The evidence for the resurrection is better than for claimed miracles in any other religion. It's outstandingly different in quality and quantity.

ANTONY FLEW
DID THE RESURRECTION HAPPEN?

O ne of the most dangerous ideas in all of human history is the notion that Jesus rose from the dead.[39] Why? Because it seriously calls the status quo into question. The belief that Jesus left the grave behind forever catapulted His followers to launch a courageous and sacrificial movement animated by the tangible hope that death need not spell the end of the human story. To our contemporary noses, though, belief in the resurrection smells of ancient superstition and wishful thinking, perhaps because it flies in the face of our everyday experience.

People do not come back from death.

Death has aptly been described as the full stop in the grand sentence of life. Our uniform observation teaches us that death seems awfully permanent. *In general,* there is no debate over whether or not dead people stay dead. That is self-evidently true. The question is whether Jesus *in particular* rose from the dead, where the singularity is the entire point.

The events of Easter lie so much at the heart of the Christian story that if Jesus did stay dead, then Christianity needs an undertaker. For if Jesus' grave is still occupied, then He was a fraud, Christianity is merely a delusion, and Christians should be pitied for being duped by false hope (see 1 Cor. 15:14–19). Suspend disbelief for a moment, though, and consider the flip side. If Jesus *did* rise from the dead, then such an anomalous event, nothing short of a miracle, surely substantiates Jesus' claim to be God and thereby establishes the core truth of the Christian story.

The stakes are high. Though even if we may wish it to be true, with so much hanging in the balance, belief in the resurrection can seem like an insurmountable intellectual obstacle. And what so often hinders people from taking the first step to investigate the historical evidence is a philosophical barrier known as the problem of miracles. For if you do not believe that miracles are even possible or that it is ever rational to believe in them, then it would make sense to dismiss the evidence for Jesus' resurrection out of hand.

So are miracles possible?

Tracing all the way back to a few enlightenment philosophers (Spinoza, Voltaire, and Hume), the problem of miracles argues that nature's regularity, established firmly by our uniform observations through science, is inviolable.[40] And since miracles are violations of the laws of nature, surely our scientific view of the world has rendered miracles impossible, for you cannot violate the inviolable. The chief problem here, though, is that the argument is circular, for it assumes that God does not exist and that therefore miracles are impossible.

While these enlightenment philosophers invented the idea that the laws of nature were ironclad, prescribing how things must happen, Christian thinkers around the same time (Galileo, Kepler, Bacon, Pascal, and Newton) followed the classical definition that spoke of the laws of nature as merely describing what normally happens, or how God normally governs the world through rational order.[41] The difference? Whether or not God exists.

For if God does exist, then there is no reason to think that the laws of nature are inviolable. Science would merely furnish our understanding as to how God normally governs the universe, where the regularity of nature is the very thing required for us to recognize when God does something different. This would mean that the laws of nature do not constrain God—they expose Him, for against the backdrop of nature's regularity, God arrests our attention when He does something miraculous.[42]

This does not mean, though, that any miracle claim should be blindly believed. Given the history of humanity too quickly ascribing supernatural explanations to natural phenomena, we should all maintain a healthy dose of skepticism. This is especially true when supposed eyewitnesses to a miracle could be deceived, deluded, or even deceivers themselves. But if we are willing to keep an open mind about God's existence, and if the purported miracle makes sense within a broader religious context (as in the case of Jesus' resurrection within the Christian story), there is no reason to dismiss the possibility of a miracle without giving the evidence a fair hearing.

So what is the historical evidence surrounding Jesus' resurrection?

Scholars of every stripe in the relevant fields unite around the conviction that four facts surrounding Jesus' death and purported resurrection are firmly established: (1) Jesus died by crucifixion under the sentence of Pontius Pilate; (2) Jesus' well-known tomb was discovered empty by a bunch of Jesus' women followers on Easter Sunday; (3) Jesus' disciples genuinely believed they saw Him physically alive again after His death; and (4) Saul of Tarsus was converted to Christianity through what he genuinely believed was an encounter with the resurrected Jesus.[43] That you have such consensus across religious and philosophical lines, including from a host of skeptical scholars who do not believe in God or miracles, suggests that these facts jump over an incredibly high bar when it comes to the historical criteria they satisfy.[44]

Of course, these facts do not prove the miraculous resurrection of Jesus. Historians are careful not to feed in causes outside of the philosophical assumptions of their field, and so mostly leave open the question as to how to explain this seemingly anomalous data. Yet these facts cry out for an explanation, as they leave a resurrection-shaped hole in history. Anyone who wants to deny that Jesus rose from the dead needs to come up with some other non-miraculous explanation to fill the void. And there are no shortage of candidates.

Perhaps the earliest attempt to refute the resurrection was the polemic leveled by some Jewish leaders against Jesus' disciples, calling them *deceivers*. The conspiracy hypothesis, or the charge that Jesus' disciples stole the body and fabricated the resurrection story, appeared so early that it was even incorporated into Matthew's gospel (Matt. 28:13). But this theory suffers from a number of challenges. For starters, one of the early sources reports that the well-known tomb was guarded by a Roman sentry to avoid exactly this kind of tampering (Matt. 27:62–66). Not to mention the fact that this theory only explains the death of Jesus and the empty tomb but does nothing to explain the post-resurrection appearances to large numbers of Jesus' followers or the conversion of Saul of Tarsus. And if the disciples stole the body and sought to fabricate a convincing story for religious propaganda, there is no way they would have allowed women to discover the empty tomb, for at that time, a woman's testimony was considered questionable at best and inadmissible at worst.[45] But the real Achilles' heel of the conspiracy theory is explaining *why* the disciples would do it.

According to N. T. Wright, an ancient historian and expert on first-century Judaism, no one at the time believed in the resurrection of one man in the middle of history.[46] The disciples' claim that Jesus rose from the dead was a spontaneous evolution of the existing Jewish belief that everyone would be resurrected to judgment at the end of history. But even if Jesus' disciples did have the theological creativity to invent the claim, they had no motivation for doing so. Shrinking back to their former lives, they could have easily lived in comfortable anonymity. Instead, the disciples faced all manner of hardship for preaching about Jesus and His resurrection, enduring opposition, ostracism, homelessness, beatings, and stoning, and all from their own people. We even have good historical evidence that at least four of the apostles were martyred, probably more, and no evidence to suggest any of them ever recanted their testimony, even under the threat of death.[47] And when you consider that saying Jesus was God was considered blasphemy by orthodox Jews, there is no conceivable sense of what the disciples stood to gain in this life or the next by lying. This is why the full gamut of critical scholars tend to agree that the disciples were not *deceivers* but that they *genuinely believed* they had seen Jesus alive. Nothing else explains what shifted their theology or ignited their courage.

Perhaps, then, the apostles were *deceived*, and Jesus did not really die in the first place. Maybe a twin brother took His place, or perhaps Jesus only swooned under the strain of the cross and then regained consciousness later to be nursed back to health. The twin theory suffers from the fact that Jesus' family was too involved in all the wrong ways for this to work. Not only did the Jewish Sanhedrin try Jesus, with plenty of people familiar with the popular teacher, but Jesus was crucified in full view of His mother. If anyone could spot an imposter on the cross or know if Jesus had a twin, it was Mary. Yet after Jesus' resurrection, Mary was heavily involved with the early church, along with Jesus' half brothers James and Jude, who before Jesus' resurrection were skeptical of Jesus' claims (Mark 3:21; John 7:5; Acts 1:14). So the twin theory suffers from the same problem as the conspiracy theory, lacking any serious motive. If Jesus' family knew the story was fake, they wouldn't suffer the lie. It also cannot explain how either Jesus or the imposter twin was able to produce the relevant scars to convince Jesus' disciples that He had risen from the dead (John 20:20–27).

The swoon theory bumps into the problem that the death of Jesus is one of the most well-documented events in ancient history.

Not only is it mentioned in Paul's early creed in 1 Corinthians, as the closest window we have into the claims around Easter, but it is mentioned in all four canonical Gospels in the New Testament, along with a host of extra-biblical and non-Christian sources.[48] No competing traditions exist that suggest Jesus either survived His crucifixion or revived in the tomb. When you consider the agony and strain Jesus' body endured with the scourging and crucifixion,[49] along with the Roman customs surrounding condemned prisoners and the expertise of the executioners in knowing when someone was dead, the swoon theory is deeply problematic. It also fails to account for the conversion of Saul of Tarsus, not to mention how a pulverized and half-dead Jesus, desperately in need of medical attention, would be able to convince His disciples that He had forever conquered death.[50] Due to this cornucopia of historical evidences, perhaps more than for any other event in ancient history, scholars resound that Jesus was definitely dead.

So what if Jesus stayed dead and the disciples were simply *deluded?* Perhaps after the psychological trauma of seeing their friend executed, they all hallucinated that they saw Him alive again. The monumental problem with this suggestion is that not even a marijuana plantation burning away on a nearby Judean hillside could account for the scope of these post-resurrection appearances. Why? Because by definition hallucinations are private mental events, not shared.[51] Except Jesus was said to appear to individuals and groups, in different locations and social settings, right across a period of forty days (Matt. 28:1–20; Luke 24:1–53; John 20:1—21:25; Acts 1:1–11). Jesus hugged people, had them touch His scars, and ate food with them. Plus, hallucinations do not tend to have an exact end date coinciding with Jesus' ascension into heaven. The final nail in the coffin of this theory is that it cannot explain the empty tomb, nor why Saul of Tarsus would have a similar hallucination, when at the time he was suffering no such grief and was intent on stamping out the Christian movement. So the hallucination thesis is also soundly rejected.

In more recent years, some have attempted to suggest that the resurrection story *developed* with time, as though a myth or legend. But the early Christian creed Paul includes in 1 Corinthians 15 is dated by even the most skeptical scholars to be within three months to at most five years after the events of the first Easter.[52] And wrapped up in that creed, you have all of our four facts, implied or explicit.[53] So the resurrection story comes incredibly early. And if one wanted to claim that a legend grew up over time for the purposes of religious propaganda, then it is exceedingly difficult to explain the shift from Paul's early creed (which only mentioned male eyewitnesses) to the four Gospels, which all came later and have women discovering the tomb. Given the status of the testimony of women in the ancient world, if you did not want to say the more developed stories in the Gospels serve deceptive or motivated ends, then these later features are exceedingly difficult to account for. So the legend thesis trips over the evidence and falls profoundly short.

So what happened?

It seems that none of these non-miraculous theories can explain all the facts surrounding the events of Easter. And if we were to set aside any presuppositions we may have about the possibility of miracles and view the situation like a jury in a court case, examining and weighing all the evidence, how should we fill the resurrection-shaped hole in history? Sherlock Holmes, the famed fictional detective, weighs in on this question: "Once one has eliminated the impossible, whatever remains, no matter how improbable, must be the truth."[54]

The evidence we have may not seem extraordinary enough for some, but there is quite a lot of it, perhaps more than nearly any other ancient event. Though we don't have the video evidence or death certificate we wish we had, what we do have is precisely the type of evidence we should expect if Jesus was, in fact, raised from the dead. As the only explanation that accounts for all the known facts, it is a rational step to embrace the resurrection of Jesus. And this is *good news*. For when we consider the painful reality of death, the resurrection of Jesus breathes a glorious hope into the lungs of an otherwise final and hopeless situation. For if Jesus triumphed over death, demoting it from a full stop to a comma in the grand sentence of life, then we can believe Him when He promises that "whoever believes in him should not perish but have eternal life" (John 3:16).

Recommended Reading

Miracles by C. S. Lewis
Miracles (2 Volumes) by Craig S. Keener
The Case for the Resurrection of Jesus by Gary Habermas and
    Michael Licona
The Resurrection of the Son of God by N. T. Wright

SEVEN

How Can God Be Good When the Church Is So Bad?

*It was reserved for Christianity to present to the world
an ideal character, which through all the changes of
eighteen centuries has inspired the hearts of men with
an impassioned love; has shown itself capable of acting
on all ages, nations, temperaments, and conditions;
has been not only the highest pattern of virtue but the
strongest incentive to its practice; and has exercised
so deep an influence that it may be truly said that the
simple record of three short years of active life has done
more to regenerate and to soften mankind than all the
disquisitions of philosophers, and all the exhortations
of moralists.*

WILLIAM LECKY
*HISTORY OF EUROPEAN MORALS
FROM AUGUSTUS TO CHARLEMAGNE*

Perhaps the biggest obstacle to belief in God in recent years has been a growing disillusionment with Christians and the church. No doubt the church has a historical closet full of skeletons. Even in our own lifetimes, horrendous evils have been exposed, with those who bear God's name having done reprehensible things under the institutional cover of the church. So with the church's moral currency bankrupted by religious hypocrisy, and when you consider that part of the Christian story supposedly involves a change brought about in the human heart by God, how do you explain Christians behaving badly?

How can God be so good when the church is so bad?

There should be no room for any answer to a question this raw that does not begin with tremendous sorrow for those who have been harmed, closely followed by a deep protest against any on-going existence of those evils. God Himself is intimately familiar with the terrible wounds that can accompany being the target of religious hypocrisy since the religious establishment, who were meant to be a spiritual safe haven, were the very ones whose dark actions of betrayal and injustice led to Jesus' brutal execution.

One of the intriguing features about the Christian story is that there is no attempt to airbrush out the unseemly reality of religious evils. Rather than sweep hypocrisy under the rug, the Bible has a habit of dragging it out into the open, where sunlight serves as the best disinfectant. Nearly every letter in the New Testament was written to address a serious shortcoming in the beliefs or behaviors of Christians who were not framing God right in the eyes of a watching world. And consider how these failures were dealt with publicly, as God memorialized these letters forever when they became Christian Scripture.

There has never been a more vocal critic of religious hypocrisy than Jesus. He spoke of some religious leaders as whitewashed tombs, exposing the hidden reality that behind any renovated exterior designed to look good in the public eye, there was an inward dimension to these figures that resembled a moral and spiritual corpse (Matt. 23:27–28). And when it comes to judgment, Jesus warned that no one will get away with anything. There is no escaping that Jesus spoke terrifying words about judgment, only these words were never aimed at secular people or pagans or notorious sinners. With deep compassion for the victims of abuse, Jesus' strongest warnings of judgment were aimed at religious people, especially religious leaders who were misrepresenting God and hurting others.

The crux of the challenge is not really whether or not Christians behave badly, which should be tragically obvious to everyone, but whether Christians behaving badly should stop you from becoming a Christian yourself. To throw out the Christian story because of these negative examples represents a leap in logic that, although perhaps understandable, tends to highlight two underlying myths popularly believed about Christians and the church.

The first myth is that church history is all bad. Were we to survey people's encounters with Christians throughout the ages, for every story of violence or abuse we would find innumerable countering stories of mercy and love. And when we zoom out to take stock of the macro perspective, the same survey would yield fascinating results. Nearly a dozen books in just the last two decades trace the riches of our cultural inheritance, the so-called *best of the west*, back to the teaching of Jesus and His followers.[55] This legacy of Jesus was an indispensable catalyst to the development of universal human rights, education and healthcare for all, women's equality, charity and welfare, modern science, non-violent resistance, limits on secular powers, and the emergence of historically unique virtues like humility. Given the sheer positive impact of Christians and the church on our culture, it is virtually unimaginable to consider what the world would be like today without Jesus' ongoing influence.

Now this is no attempt to excuse the evils done by those who claim to follow Christ. Those deeds have been horribly destructive. Rather, what we are trying to do is draw a wedge between Jesus and these evils, to show that you cannot draw a straight line from any of Jesus' teaching to the dark deeds of the church. Quite the opposite. The problem isn't that these people were being Christian, the problem is that they weren't being Christian enough.

To spell out this point, our friend and historian John Dickson used the metaphor of a musical score.[56] With His life, Jesus masterfully composed a sublime piece of music about what living with and for God looks like, and Christians are the amateurs learning to play the tune. Throughout history, sometimes Jesus followers have got it right, and other times they have been dreadfully off-key or have walked away from the score altogether. What determines the quality of the music, though, is not the poor performance of a learner. You should never judge a belief by its abuse. The only way to evaluate a score is to see, when played correctly, whether it makes for a divine harmony. So far from poisoning everything, church history highlights countless instances where, following in the legacy of Jesus, Christians have lived beautiful lives and, in so doing, have bequeathed to the world an array of benefits.

The second myth that needs debunking is the notion that all Christians are hypocrites. Undoubtedly there are some for whom the label fits, but if Christians really believed the gospel, then there should be no Christian hypocrites. The word *hypocrite* comes from the ancient world of stage performers. Hypocrites were actors, characters who wore a mask, people who were privately one thing and publicly, on show to the world, another personality altogether. That is the essence of hypocrisy: to present a carefully curated image or brand to the public world that looks nothing like your private self.

The myth that all Christians are hypocrites stems from the wrong assumption that to become a Christian is to instantly become a good person. The Christian story says the reverse is true. We are not good people. Sure, humans were *created for good*, but according to the Christian story, we are all now *damaged by evil*, living in the shadow of the fall. Jesus' diagnosis is that we all fall short of the way of love, and that left to our own, we too are moral and spiritual corpses. That is why we need a Savior.

There is no hypocrisy in claiming publicly that there is a right way to live under God's design that leads to our freedom and flourishing and life, and then unfortunately fail to live up to it, so long as we don't publicly pretend that we do live up to it. As sinful people saved by God's grace rather than by our own good works, there should be no need for the public pretense of perfection. The truth that we desperately need God's new mercies each and every morning should breed a deep humility and transparency in the public lives of Christians.

If anything, Christians behaving badly lends strength to one of the central claims of the Christian story: that all people, Christians included, are seriously flawed. If we are going to reject becoming a Christian because of a questionable history of bad behavior in the church, then we had also better be consistent and reject being a human being altogether, for the only thing worse than church history is the rest of human history.

That Christians do behave badly is a tragedy, though it shows God's consistency to His endgame. Since creating loving and responsible creatures has always been God's goal, freedom remains the way, meaning that Christians are free to wander off script, hurt others, and damage the reputation of the church. But as messy as the church is, and despite any perception that the church is beyond saving, Jesus loves the church. He is committed to making her beautiful and a beacon of hope for the world. And who knows? Perhaps your own sense of protest aligns with God's heart of correction, and you might have a powerful contribution to make in shaping the future of the church for good.

Recommended Reading

For the Love of God: How the Church Is Better and Worse Than You Ever Imagined by Natasha Moore with John Dickson, Simon Smart, and Justine Toh
Doubters Guide to the Church by John Dickson
The Book That Made Your World by Vishal Mangalwadi
Dominion by Tom Holland

The Adventure
Awaits

It's a dangerous business, Frodo, going out your door. . . .
You step into the Road, and if you don't keep your feet,
there is no knowing where you might be swept off to.

J. R. R. TOLKIEN
THE FELLOWSHIP OF THE RING

There is something wondrous about this adventure we all find ourselves in. What we have tried to do over the course of this book is to show how the Christian story sheds light on this enchantment and how the deep things we all love and long for are more than mere illusions. At some point along our own personal journeys, we became gripped by this story. Jesus' answers to life's deepest questions mapped on to the soulish contours of our experience in a way that made sense. And with our questions welcomed from the beginning, we found that asking away at the Christian story only led to a greater confidence that Christianity stands up under scrutiny. After long years of believing in and following Jesus, around all the twists and dips in the road, we can honestly say that we have found ourselves by losing ourselves in the story.

There was a time when statements like these would have seemed strange to our own ears. You may still have questions that hold you back, or you may be nervous to take the step because you don't know where it leads. Search. Question. Scrutinize. Weigh information. Take the time you need to make a decision you can bank on, for God is never in a hurry.

Our closing word to you is that experiencing God personally is what ultimately made the story worth embracing. With seasons marked by sacrifice and suffering, and others buoyed by laughter and goodness, we have found rich meaning and help and hope in following Jesus. And perhaps the most exciting aspect of becoming a Christian, of joining Jesus on the road, is the unpredictability of God. For it is when you hand over the pen of your own life story that you find yourself swept up into an adventure as wild as the imagination of God.

Notes

WHY READ THIS BOOK?

1. The language for our six-scene framework is adapted from David Benson, "Schools, scripture, and secularization," PhD thesis, University of Queensland, April 9, 2016, https://espace.library.uq.edu.au/view /UQ:384064, and a fourfold framework (*designed for good, damaged by evil, restored for better, sent to heal*) from Steve Choung, *True Story: A Christianity Worth Believing In* (Westmont, IL: InterVarsity Press, 2008).

THE GARDEN: CREATED FOR GOOD

2. C. S. Lewis, *Mere Christianity* (London: Williams Collins, 2013), 161–62.

A NEW RELATIONSHIP

3. Pete Grieg, *How to Pray: A Simple Guide for Normal People* (Colorado Springs: NavPress, 2019).

A NEW WAY TO LIVE

4. John Dickson, *A Doubter's Guide to Jesus: An Introduction to the Man from Nazareth for Believers and Skeptics* (New York: HarperCollins, 2018), chapter 3.
5. Confucius, *The Analects*, trans. D. C. Lau (London: Penguin Books, 1979), 15.24.
6. Luke 6:31.

THE DOORWAY OF DOUBT

7. See Jonathan Haidt, *The Righteous Mind: Why Good People Are Divided by Politics and Religion* (New York: Penguin, 2012), 32–60.

WHAT IF THE SNAKE WAS RIGHT?

8. For an extended treatment of the Moral Argument, see William Lane Craig, *Reasonable Faith: Christian Truth and Apologetics*, 3rd ed. (Wheaton, IL: Crossway, 2008), 172–83.

HOW COULD A GOOD GOD ALLOW SUFFERING?

9. Lactantius, "A Treatise on the Anger of God" in A. Roberts and J. Donaldson, eds., *Ante-Nicene Fathers*, vol. 7 (Peabody, MA: Hendrickson Publishers), 271.
10. David Hume, *Dialogues Concerning Natural Religion* (Cambridge, UK: Cambridge University Press, 2007), part 10.
11. See also Hebrews 6:18 and Titus 1:2.
12. For an extended treatment of the Free Will Defense, see Alvin Plantinga, *God, Freedom, and Evil* (Grand Rapids: Eerdmans, 1974).

WHY ISN'T GOD MORE OBVIOUS?

13. Jerry Walls and Trent Dougherty, eds., *Two Dozen (or so) Arguments for God: The Plantinga Project* (Oxford: Oxford University Press, 2018).
14. Friedrich Nietzsche, *Thus Spake Zarathustra* (New York: Penguin, 1964).
15. For Plantinga's seminal lecture and the work it has sparked in the philosophy of religion, see Jerry Walls and Trent Dougherty, eds., *Two Dozen (or so) Arguments for God: The Plantinga Project* (Oxford: Oxford University Press, 2018). See also Richard Swinburne, *Is There A God?* (Oxford: Oxford University Press, 2010) and William Lane Craig, *Reasonable Faith: Christian Truth and Apologetics*, 3rd ed. (Wheaton, IL: Crossway, 2008).
16. Quentin Smith, "The Metaphilosophy of Naturalism," *Philo* 4, no. 2 (2001): 195–215.
17. For the evidence and implications to the Kalam Cosmological Argument, see William Lane Craig, *Reasonable Faith: Christian Truth and Apologetics*, 3rd ed. (Wheaton, IL: Crossway, 2008), 111–56.
18. For evidence and implications to the Fine-Tuning Argument, see Luke Barnes and Allen Hainline, "The Cosmic Coincidences of Fine Tuning"

in Paul M. Gould and Daniel Ray, eds., *The Story of the Cosmos: How the Heavens Declare the Glory of God* (Eugene, OR: Harvest House Publishers, 2019), 203–19.

19. For evidence and implications, see John Lennox, *God's Undertaker: Has Science Buried God?* (Oxford: Lion Books, 2009), 135–62.

20. See Jonathan Haidt, *The Righteous Mind: Why Good People Are Divided by Politics and Religion* (New York: Penguin, 2012), 32–60.

21. Søren Kierkegaard, *Parables of Kierkegaard*, Thomas C. Oden, ed. (Princeton: Princeton University Press, 1978), 40.

22. David Bowden, *When God Isn't There: Why God Is Farther than You Think but Closer than You Dare Imagine* (Nashville: Nelson Books, 2016), 14–16.

HAS SCIENCE DISPROVED GOD?

23. Baruch A. Shalev, *100 Years of Nobel Prizes* (Delhi: Atlantic Publishers & Distributors, 2003), 57–59.

24. See Rodney Stark, *For the Glory of God: How Monotheism Led to Reformations, Science, Witch-Hunts, and the End of Slavery* (Princeton: Princeton University Press, 2003), 121–200.

25. Johannes Kepler, "Letter to Johannes Georg Herwart von Hohenburg," quoted in Christopher Kaiser, *Toward a Theology of Scientific Endeavour: The Descent of Science* (Farnham, UK: Ashgate, 2007), 144.

26. I. B. Cohen, ed., *Isaac Newton's Papers and Letters on Natural Philosophy* (Cambridge, MA: Harvard University Press, 1958), 280.

27. C. S. Lewis, *Miracles* (Glasgow, UK: Collins Publishing, 1947), 110.

28. See William Lane Craig, *Reasonable Faith: Christian Truth and Apologetics*, 3rd ed. (Wheaton, IL: Crossway, 2008), 111–56.

29. See Luke Barnes and Allan Hainline, "The Cosmic Coincidences of Fine-Tuning," in Paul M. Gould and Daniel Ray, eds., *The Story of the Cosmos: How the Heavens Declare the Glory of God* (Eugene, OR: Harvest House Publishers, 2019), 203–219. See also William Lane Craig, *Reasonable Faith*, 3rd ed. (Wheaton, IL: Crossway, 2008), 157–72.

30. Eugene Wigner, "The Unreasonable Effectiveness of Mathematics in the Natural Sciences," *Communications on Pure and Applied Mathematics*, vol. 13, no. I (February 1960).

31. John Lennox, *God's Undertaker: Has Science Buried God?* (Oxford: Lion Books, 2009), 135–61.

32. *The Story of God*, Netflix, January 3, 2017.

CAN I TRUST THE BIBLE?

33. For a list of examples, see Kenneth A. Kitchen, *On the Reliability of the Old Testament* (Grand Rapids: Eerdmans, 2006).

34. Daniel Wallace, *Revisiting the Corruption of the New Testament: Manuscript, Patristic, and Apocryphal Evidence* (Grand Rapids: Kregel Academic, 2011).

35. Richard Baukham, *Jesus and the Eyewitnesses: The Gospels as Eyewitness Testimony* (Grand Rapids: Eerdmans, 2006). See also Craig Blomberg, *The Historical Reliability of the New Testament: Countering the Challenges to Evangelical Christian Beliefs* (Nashville: B&H Publishing, 2016).

36. F. F. Bruce, *The Canon of Scripture* (Westmont, IL: InterVarsity Press, 1988).

37. One of the earliest examples of ancient graffiti was discovered on a wall near Palatine Hill in Rome. The famed *Alexaminos Graffito* depicts a man worshiping someone on a cross, who has the body of a man and the head of a donkey. Intended to mock, the image reads in Greek: "Alexaminos worships his god." See Paul's argument in 1 Corinthians 1:23 that the Cross is "a stumbling block to Jews and foolishness to Gentiles."

38. Sean McDowell, *The Fate of the Apostles: Examining the Martyrdom Accounts of the Closest Followers of Jesus* (Philadelphia: Routledge, 2015), and Michael Licona, *The Resurrection of Jesus: A New Historiographical Approach* (Westmont, IL: InterVarsity Press, 2010), 366–70.

DID JESUS REALLY RISE FROM THE DEAD?

39. Peter Hitchens, "Q&A Festival of Dangerous Ideas 2013," Australian Broadcast Corporation, November 4, 2013.

40. See for example Voltaire (1764), "Philosophical Dictionary," in *The Works of Voltaire*, vol. 11 (Paris: E. R. DuMont, 1901), 272.

41. Nancy Frankenberry, *The Faith of Scientists in Their Words* (Princeton: Princeton University Press, 2008), IX.

42. See C. S. Lewis, *Miracles: A Preliminary Study* (Glasgow, UK: Collins, 2012), 87–98.

43. For a detailed survey of the relevant scholars and the historical criteria satisfied by the facts in question, see Michael Licona, *The Resurrection of Jesus: A New Historiographical Approach* (Westmont, IL: InterVarsity Press, 2010), 302–463.

44. Gary Habermas and Michael Licona, *The Case for the Resurrection of Jesus* (Grand Rapids: Kregel, 2004), 36–40.

45. Michael Licona, *The Resurrection of Jesus: A New Historiographical Approach* (Westmont, IL: InterVarsity Press, 2010), 349–55.

46. N. T. Wright, *The Resurrection of the Son of God* (Minneapolis: Fortress Press, 2003), 146–206.

47. Sean McDowell, *The Fate of the Apostles: Examining the Martyrdom Accounts of the Closest Followers of Jesus* (Philadelphia: Routledge, 2015).

48. Flavius Josephus (*Antiquities*, 18.3), Tacitus (*Annals*, 15.44), Seutonius (*Lives of the Caesars, Claudius* Section 25 and *Nero* Section 16), Julius Africanus (*Chronography*, Book 18), Lucian of Samosata (*The Death of Peregrine*, 11), Mara Bar Serapion (*Syriac Manuscript*, Additional 14, 658), Pliny the Younger (*Letters to Trajan*), Babylonian Talmud (vol. 3, Sanhedrin 43a).

49. W. D. Edwards, W. J. Gabel, and F. E. Hosmer, "On the Physical Death of Jesus Christ," *Journal of the American Medical Association* 255, no. 11 (1986): 1455–63.

50. David F. Strauss, *The Life of Jesus for the People*, vol. 1 (London: Williams and Norgate, 1879), 412.

51. Gary Habermas, "Explaining Away Jesus' Resurrection: The Recent Revival of Hallucination Theories," *Christian Research Journal* 23, no.4 (2001).

52. See Gerd Lüdemann, *The Resurrection of Jesus: History, Experience, Theology*, trans. J. Bowden (Minneapolis: Fortress, 1994), 38.

53. 1 Corinthians 15:3–8: "For what I received I passed on to you as of first importance: that Christ died for our sins according to the Scriptures, that he was buried, that he was raised on the third day according to the Scriptures, and that he appeared to Cephas, and then to the Twelve. After that, he appeared to more than five hundred of the brothers and sisters at the same time, most of whom are still living, though some have fallen asleep. Then he appeared to James, then to all the apostles, and last of all he appeared to me also, as to one abnormally born."

54. Sir Arthur Conan Doyle, *The Sign of Four* (Durham, UK: Aziloth Books, 2010).

HOW CAN GOD BE GOOD
WHEN THE CHURCH IS SO BAD?

55. Alvin Schmidt, *How Christianity Changed the World* (Grand Rapids: Zondervan, 2004); Dinesh D'Souza, *What's So Great about Christianity?*

(Washington, DC: Regnery, 2007); Greg Sheridan, *God Is Good for You* (Sydney: Allen & Unwin, 2018); Jeremiah J. Johnstone, *Unimaginable: What Our World Would Be Like without Christianity* (Minneapolis: Bethany House Publishers, 2017); Jonathan Hill, *What Has Christianity Ever Done for Us?: How It Shaped the Modern World* (Westmont, IL: InterVarsity Press, 2005); Rodney Stark, *The Victory of Reason: How Christianity Led to Freedom, Capitalism and Western Success* (New York: Random House, 2006), Tom Holland, *Dominion* (New York: Basic Books, 2019); Vishal Mengalwadi, *The Book That Made Your World: How the Bible Created the Soul of Western Civilization* (Nashville: Thomas Nelson, 2011).

56. John Dickson, quoted in "For the Love of God: How the Church Is Better and Worse than You Ever Imagined," CPX (Center for Public Christianity, 2020), https://www.publicchristianity.org/fortheloveofgod/.